T0208927

Other books by Deanna Hurtubise

Children's Picture Books

So Many Hugs
A Guardian Angel's Lesson

Children's Historic Fiction

The Boys Who Discovered Yesterday
Felix and Belakana, Children of the Druid
Clovis and Clothilda, The Unlikely Tale of a
Teenage Warrior and His Princess
Saints Alive, Annie's Very Own Miracle

Memoire

In Sickness and in Health, A wife/caregiver
reflects on the words before I do

UNTIL DEATH.... AND THEN WHAT?

Reflections on the new path ahead

Deanna Hurtubise

WESTBOW
PRESS®
A DIVISION OF THOMAS NELSON
& ZONDERVAN

WestBow Press books may be ordered through booksellers or by contacting:

WestBow Press
A Division of Thomas Nelson & Zondervan
1663 Liberty Drive
Bloomington, IN 47403
www.westbowpress.com
1 (866) 928-1240

ISBN: 978-1-9736-9533-2 (sc)
ISBN: 978-1-9736-9534-9 (hc)
ISBN: 978-1-9736-9532-5 (e)

Library of Congress Control Number: 2020911732

Print information available on the last page.

WestBow Press rev. date: 7/27/2020

DEDICATION

To my parents for all the love given and the lessons learned
which have seen me through the good times and the bad.

CONTENTS

INTRODUCTION

When I sat down to write this collection of thoughts on widowhood, I had absolutely no idea where the chapters would take me. This was all uncharted territory. All I knew when I slipped into the frightening funk after the second anniversary of my husband's death was that I had to do something to help myself climb out of it. Rather than spending money on counseling, writing became my therapy. I had to reexamine my new station in life in more detail; I had to analyze my feelings, rethink various concepts regarding widowhood and how I was or was not truly dealing with them. It was an intense six months of self-reflection. Now, seventeen chapters later, as I look back on what I have written, to the reflections and discoveries I have made, I feel better about my new chapter. These insights aren't meant to be a tutorial on grieving; we each do it in our own way. Rather they are the result of a personal examination of how I have come to look at this uncharted path to a new normal of peace and happiness with the hopes that they could help someone else.

-One-

TRANSITION

All I can say is grief has a way of totally messing up your schedule! The last years of caring for my husband of fifty years were years of twenty-four-seven care which was impossibly difficult, I became a mega organizer. Not that I wasn't always an organized person; being a high school teacher for twenty-five years taught me decades ago that every day, every hour had to be scheduled and organized almost to the minute. Lesson plans took hours on the weekend and had to be done in such a detailed way so that they passed the inspection of the administration on Monday. Working full time and still being a wife and a mother to three children didn't offer much choice other than to be organized. But being a caregiver to another person who can never be left alone, even after retirement had become a welcomed way of life, was another thing entirely.

My husband, Paul, suffered from Parkinson's disease, heart disease and asthma. The twenty-four-seven caregiving occurred after he had broken the shelf of his femur in a fall. Twelve weeks in a rehab facility allowed him to walk again with a walker but never unattended. Never again in his life would he be permitted to walk from one room to another without someone alongside of him. That person would have to be me. This came as a total shock, and I didn't know how I was going to manage it. I lasted one year before I said "uncle" and asked for help from a palliative hospice care company which saved my sanity. At least with their scheduled visits, I could take a shower, get to the grocery store or take the dog for a walk without being in fight-or-flight mode.

My husband died three years after the leg break from congestive heart failure. We knew his time was running out, and I made all the necessary arrangements for him to die peacefully at home under the incredible care of hospice. During the three years of this total care, I began writing a journal detailing the health journey we had been on throughout our entire marriage. The journey had been extensive and stressful for the entire family. I had never intended for it to become a published book, but somehow it took on a life of its own. I finished the last chapter the morning after he died. *In Sickness and Health, A Wife/Caregiver Reflects on the words "Before I Do"*, was a labor of love to be sure, and in retrospect helped me to cope through those most difficult years.

I dwelt on the question people asked me frequently: Which is more difficult, losing someone suddenly to a heart attack or watching someone die slowly over years, allowing time to prepare for the inevitable? There really is no good answer to that question, because no two people react to death and grief the same way. I had had the experience of both when my father died suddenly from a ruptured aneurysm and then when my husband lingered for years, his health deteriorating slowly. I learned that any manner of death unhesitatingly takes a piece of the heart of those left behind, and we all just learn to cope however we can. There are no lesson plans for this!

There was one positive note to experiencing the latter in that it did give me time to prepare for whatever would come next. I have always been a list maker, and I had so many lists by the time my husband died you would have thought I could handle anything. I had decided early on that I would not want to stay in the big family house, so I had copious lists on what to do to get it cleaned out, repaired, staged, organized and ready to put on the market. I had financial lists, insurance lists, lists of people to contact, and lists of those who would need a copy of the death certificate. I couldn't believe it when the funeral director advised me to have ten copies! I wondered why so many, but he was right. One list I neglected to make was a list of health concerns of my own and how to deal with them. For three years I had done next to nothing to take care of myself, self-diagnosing whatever symptom I was experiencing rather than going to a doctor. That would have meant paying someone to stay with my husband! It didn't take long after his death for that to change, and I ended up needing medical attention. Turns out my self-diagnosis over the years had been totally wrong, and I was relieved to finally have the matter taken care of easily and correctly.

So within a few weeks of his funeral in August, my lists got tackled in a fury of activity. I had made a deadline for how many months I would need before putting a For Sale sign in the yard. The deadline was March 1. The house was so big, so empty, and so depressing; his presence was everywhere, and I felt that I had to get out as soon as possible. I weighed the emotion of having to leave the place where so many happy memories had occurred, the family holidays, the birthday parties, the patio parties, the dinner parties for friends and colleagues, with the emotion of having to stay in the place where so much illness, caregiving and grief had occurred. The former, I found, was not enough to convince me to stay. It was a big house, and it needed a family. It needed children to fill all the empty rooms. It had been a perfect house at one time, filling all our family needs. But now those needs had changed.

I realize now that my hamster-on-a-wheel frenzy probably helped me get through the early stages of grief. I look back now two years later and see an obsessed woman on a mission to survive. I worked tirelessly every day from August, 2017 to March, 2018 deciding what to keep, what to give away and what to throw away. It took five weeks just to clear out my husband's home office. I always knew he was a pack rat, but this was ridiculous. I shredded tax documents and cancelled checks in boxes from thirty-five years ago until I actually broke the shredder! There were thirteen book shelves in this room, and most of their occupants were not going with me wherever I moved. As a scientist, my husband had amassed a wealth of medical tomes, one heavier than the next, and I found to my dismay, that no one wanted them. Libraries wouldn't take them, and they had to be thrown away! He had saved literally hundreds of old medical journals, some still in their plastic wrappers, and they, too, all had to be thrown away.

One closet at a time, one room after another got checked off my lists. The entire fall and winter had passed in a frenzy of activity; trips to Good Will, trips to the library to donate hundreds of books; it never seemed to end. We had lived in that house for thirty-one years, and there was a lot to get rid of. I wasn't prepared, however, for a new list of things that needed attention after the house inspector got finished. I couldn't believe the picky little things he found as well as some of the bigger, more expensive repairs that had to be addressed before the sign could go in the yard. That was a list I didn't enjoy making! Somehow, it all got done, I had lost a few pounds, and the bank account had slimmed down even more than I had, but the time had finally come after seven exhausting months to sell the last home my husband and I had shared. The sign went in the yard on March 1.

It was particularly difficult to watch the reactions of the eight grandchildren. They loved that house; it was like their second home, and I hoped and prayed that whatever house I bought, they would find their favorite spaces and come to love it, too. The last Christmas there was very poignant. The elephant in the room was the empty chair where the kids' Papa had always sat and had given out the gifts. One of Paul's brothers had told me that when they were all children, the youngest always picked one gift and gave it to the recipient. Everyone watched as it was opened. That person, then, would pick the next and give it out, and on and on it went till all the presents had been opened. So I decided to repeat this procedure in Paul's honor on that first Christmas without him. It seemed to help get rid of the elephant. Then one of the children said, "I'm really going to miss this house, especially at Christmas." All I could say was, "Me, too."

We had sold two previous homes when we were younger, one

selling in just thirty-five days to a Chinese family who chose it because the front door faced the east and the other in just a couple of months. They had both been relatively easy experiences, even with having young children still at home. But I can honestly say I didn't anticipate how crazy and stressful this third experience would be. Then I realized this time I was doing it alone, not to mention that I was thirty-one years older. There was no husband to be a part of all the work. For some reason it never occurred to me during the previous seven months that I was doing everything alone. I didn't think about it; I just did it. But now the house had to be in perfect and showable condition at any and all hours of the day. There would be times when I would be lucky to have a half hour notice to have every room perfect, staged appropriately, lighting just so, and the dog and me gone. On one occasion I was given fifteen minutes! Even with the organized morning routine I devised and followed religiously to prepare, fifteen minutes was not fun. Since I couldn't leave the dog in the house, I had to figure out what to do with her for the hour I was required to be away. I couldn't go shopping; if it was raining I couldn't take her to the park for a walk. It was really a hassle. Granted, it was not a third world country problem, but it was still stressful. Some days I just drove around looking for houses for sale. Other days, I would sit in my car in my neighbor's driveway where the dog and I had many conversations about the state of our lives during these stake outs. On one occasion as I was in the neighbor's driveway talking with them instead of the dog, suddenly the mother of the family looking at my house walked across the street to ask us more about the neighborhood. Of course, she had no idea it was my house she was considering.

My son was my realtor, and that was really a blessing. He took me to all the houses I wanted to see. I went to open houses almost every weekend and searched the internet daily for every house on the market in my area. My biggest fear was that someone would see my house, fall in love with it early on, make a generous offer I couldn't refuse, leaving me with no place to go. And that almost happened.

In January when I was still clearing out my house, I found a house online that I loved and which spoke to me. When there was an open house scheduled, I went to see it. Only two miles from my present home, it was conveniently located to everything, was in a lovely neighborhood, and had a beautiful yard and gardens that looked great in the online photos. It was so pretty, it looked to me like a fairy tale house. It had been the model home in the subdivision thirty-six years ago, so the landscaping was beautiful and mature. Of course this was the dead of winter so the gardens didn't look much like the photos, but the potential was there. It had most of the features I either needed or just wanted, and I asked my son to arrange a showing. The good news was that it was affordable, unoccupied and had been empty for a while, so we didn't have to worry about anyone's schedule.

I couldn't wait to get back inside. I was totally shocked when my son tried to talk me out of it. "Mom, I'm not feeling this for you. I think you're settling for the first thing you see because you're afraid of not having a place to go." I knew there were things that were dated in a thirty-six year old house, but that didn't bother me. I mean really, I was dated, too! If I got a good price for my house, I would be able to afford the upgrades. But he said I could do better. So back online I went looking for a house that would meet his approval. He was the professional, after all! I get upset with myself now that I didn't trust my own judgment. Was he right? Was I too afraid to be homeless to wait for the perfect house? I talked to my departed husband daily, asking him to help me get this right. I prayed like never before to make the pieces of the puzzles come together.

January came and went as did February, and I admit I had a lump in my throat when I saw the For Sale sign staring at me on March 1. In the beginning there were lots of lookers but no offers.

Out of curiosity I went online every day to see if my fairy tale house was still available, and it always was. Then my son and I went to another house he had found and thought would be perfect for me. It was a cute ranch with everything updated and move-in ready. He thought I should limit my looking to one floor homes so as not to have to deal with stairs. I agreed that a ranch would be ideal, but just how old did he think I was? Besides, any ranch I saw that I loved was too expensive, and anything I could afford was too small. He tried to convince me that this refurbished ranch was my perfect house, and he almost succeeded. But there was no way to do anything about it until my house sold. I checked every day and it stayed on the market for weeks, but then one day when I looked, the listing said "Sale pending". I was heartsick, and I had to start all over hunting for the next perfect house. Meanwhile, my fairy tale house was still available. I drove over to see it multiple times, parked across the street and just looked at it, trying to picture myself living there. Sometimes I took the dog with me, and we walked all around the empty house looking in windows as I tried to figure out where my furniture would go. One day the dog and I sat on a built-in bench on the deck in the snow and talked about it.

"What do you think about this yard?" I asked her. "Do you think you'd like it here? We'd have to have a fence built for you." She wagged her tail which I took as a yes. In retrospect, I'm surprised no one called the police about this lady who was stalking the house. I went to another open house, my third time inside, and took my daughter to see it, and she had the same reaction as her brother. What in the world was wrong with this house? Why didn't anyone else like it when it spoke to me so strongly? And so I kept on searching.

My son explained to me early on that there were three distinct scenarios which could unfold.

1. Someone would buy my house before I had a place to go. I would have to put everything in storage and rent somewhere till I found a house. Not an option in my opinion. Not with a dog.

2. I would find a house I wanted before mine was sold and possibly have two mortgages for however long it took to sell my house, and given the fact that there had been no offers to this point, that didn't seem like a smart option

in my opinion. I was not a risk taker where finances were concerned.

3. No one would ever make an offer on my house, and I would have to stay in my big, empty, depressing house forever. This was definitely not an option in my mind at this time in my life.

"There has to be fourth option!" I cried.

"And what would that be?" he asked.

"Someone will buy my house, I'll find a house I love and have plenty of time to leave one and move into the other." I answered hopefully.

"Yes, and miracles do happen!" he said. "Really, Mom, that rarely ever happens."

March came and went and my own extensive perennial gardens were shaping up to show well. It was the first spring I didn't spend a fortune on annual flowers, and I hated that. This yard no longer felt like mine. I know it sounds silly, but I felt like a gardener without a garden, and it made me melancholy.

After several Open Houses produced comments like, "too dated" and "priced too high for the updates needed" my son and I decided to lower the price. That produced more traffic, and I continued my frantic search for a home. Nothing ever appealed to me, some were just ok, and I was beginning to worry that I'd never find the right house.

April rolled around and by mid-month, I finally received an offer! After doing the offer/counter offer dance for two, we settled on a price. The problem was, if I accepted the offer I had to be packed, moved and into another house in thirty days! I didn't think that was even remotely possible since I hadn't even packed one box. Suddenly my son's option #1 was looking like a reality. The dog and I would have to put everything in storage and rent someplace for who knew how long? I accepted her offer and went into panic mode, packed like a crazy woman, had heavy boxes sitting in practically every room and in my almost non-existent spare time, continued to go house hunting. I had to schedule another inspection, but I had tackled so many things from an earlier pre-sale inspection I felt confident that there would be no further issues.

Since I was determined to not rent anywhere, I drove my son crazy taking me to one house after another. I finally found a nice two story whose seller also had boxes sitting everywhere and was totally fine with having to vacate in a hurry. Perhaps it was meant to be, I thought. It wasn't my perfect house but timing was everything, and I made an offer she accepted.

Just when I began to breathe deeply again, the worst thing that could have happened did. When my buyer saw the inspector's list of things still needing to be done, she backed out of the deal completely, leaving me with my house in total disarray just as I had to put it back on the market. Of course, this meant I had to back out of the offer I made on the other house. I really hated to do that. But the good news was I had averted renting at least for a while!

The month of May brought another offer that was too much of an insult to even consider at all, and by the middle of the month a third offer came that looked promising. It was from a family with five children who fell in love with everything they saw. I felt good about having kids playing in that gorgeous yard, enjoying the awesome spacious interior with all those five bedrooms filled with little ones again, and I imagined their joy at their first Christmas there. And the best news was that they weren't in a hurry to move in. I had a buyer!

About this same time, my fairy tale house had another Open House. This time I took my sister along for another pair of eyes. I called my son and told him that I was going to probably make an offer on the house he didn't like. I told him I knew he thought I was settling and that he wasn't feeling it for me, but I was feeling it, and that was the end of the discussion! My sister agreed it was a wonderful house and wondered, too, why no one else though it was right for me. It had been on the market such a long time, and the price had continued to fall making it a great deal for me. Suddenly, my rare and miraculous option #4 was playing out. I closed on the new house and had five weeks to gradually do all the updates necessary, get a fence installed for the dog and move things at my leisure. Well, not leisure exactly. It was the hardest work I had ever done to this point. I packed my little VW Beetle to the brim four or five times a day and hauled everything I could physically lift into the new house before going back for more. I was exhausted, but it was a good tired knowing my fairy tale house had waited for me. My son-in-law had been our mortgage banker, and he did some creative financing that limited a double mortgage to only one month! Those weeks of loading the car daily gave me time to tackle the updates needed, the new kitchen appliances, an interior paint job, a fence for the dog, and new carpet on the screen porch. Option #4 was working out perfectly. I had gotten my miracle! When I think back to this frantic time in my life, I can remember having only three inconsolable fits of sobbing. Only three times that I gave in to the grief; I guess I just didn't give myself time to do more than that. Was that healthy or was it escaping the inevitable? Who knows? Is there really any one way to grieve?

-Two-
GIFTS

It was a restless night, the last one at this house. The alarm screamed the beginning of the remaining few hours in this beautiful home, and I knew it was going to be an exhausting day. I had done all I could do to prepare for the movers who would arrive bright and early. As I tried to focus my eyes still tired from the lack of sleep in this bedroom I had once loved, my first thoughts were *right over there is where he died, where he had spoken his last words to me in a voice so weak it was hard to hear.* "Boy, you sure look pretty," he had said from his hospital bed. I had to laugh since I needed a shower badly, wore no makeup and was wearing baggy clothes that hung on me after losing nearly thirty pounds. He was always a soft spoken man who rarely raised his voice in anger. There was a calming quality to it that usually put everyone at ease around him. His Parkinson's disease had robbed him little by little of the volume needed to be heard easily, but I'd have given anything to hear it one more time. It was one year ago that he told me he was "checking out" letting me know he was ready to stop fighting all his health demons. Now I was checking out of this house for good. After the final packing of the last few boxes, final cleaning, final walk with the dog on this street and saying goodbye to good neighbors, final chapter here, the time had come at last to move on. I knew I would never return. The movers arrived on time bringing with them the threat of an all-day rain, but after a most heartfelt chat with God begging Him to hold off the bad weather, He complied. The four young men worked at a non-stop pace, efficiently and methodically and not wasting any time yet chatting lightheartedly about Star Wars and every other action packed movie they had seen. They were muscular and strong and looked so very young.

As each room emptied of furniture, I took broom or vacuum cleaner in hand to ready the space for the new family. Suddenly dog toys lost long ago appeared from under furniture, and a few of my husband's prescription drugs that had rolled under his recliner chair after he had dropped them without my knowing it showed up again inside balls of dust. This once vibrant and happy house echoed with its emptiness. It was suddenly devoid of personality, a shell of what it had been for three decades, a beautiful shell, but a shell nonetheless.

When the movers finished five hours later, they asked me to walk through one more time to be sure nothing had been left behind. I really didn't want to do this, but their rules required it. Each empty space triggered a memory; the bedroom where he died with the entire family surrounding him, the bathroom where the Hospice nurse helped him shower until he could no longer walk there, the play room and the "butterfly room" which the grandchildren named because of the decor, the two rooms where the eight of them always congregated, laughed, talked and thought up shows to perform for the adults. I continued on to the living room, the space where thirty-one Christmas celebrations had taken place, the dining room, home to countless birthdays, Thanksgiving and Christmas dinners, the kitchen where the kids' table held joyous giggling and conversations and where he and I had played our favorite board game up until the week before he died. I walked into the family room, once a favorite space and where he spent most of his last days, this room left vacant in the last year; I just couldn't go in there anymore. I was immediately reminded of the hummingbird that tapped on the family room window every night for the first three nights after he died. It was the only one I had seen all year. Somehow I wasn't surprised when I researched the symbolism of hummingbirds and discovered they symbolize resurrection. I went downstairs to the pool table room where the older grandkids were just beginning to learn to play and where they all decorated their own "grandchildren Christmas tree" every year. I walked through the bar where so many Happy Hours had been spent with family and friends and where we had thrown our last big party for our fiftieth wedding anniversary just a year ago. Was that really only a year ago? It felt like so much longer. I walked into his office where he had spent countless hours preparing lectures for his medical students but where he sat with his eyes closed most of the time in his last year of life. I checked out my office where I wrote lesson plans and graded papers and where I wrote my first children's books after I retired. I walked out to the wonderfully inviting patio where we spent every day of his last spring and summer, he in his wheelchair while I sat on the swing reading to him, listening to the gentle sounds of the fountain and all the bird songs. The spectacular gardens I had created over the decades looked so beautiful at this time of year; I really did hate to leave them. I ran my hand over the lid of the hot tub which he gave me for my fiftieth birthday and which I used all year around. There was nothing like it in winter when it was snowing and the steam rose off the water. This final walk through was memory overload, almost too much to bear at the moment. It was like I wasn't just saying goodbye to my home; I was saying goodbye to him all over again. I was saying goodbye to an important chapter of my life. I had known this day would be difficult; I knew I didn't want to stay there, but I wasn't prepared for this crushing wave of sadness.

As the movers took the final boxes from the garage, I began sweeping it and noticed a piece of loose leaf paper, folded in threes in the middle of the floor. It was wrinkled and dirty, and I could see my name written on the outside in my husband's handwriting. *What in the world is this?* I thought, picked it up and opened it. Inside was a letter he had written to me dated April, 1987, the month we had bought this house. It was titled "All the Things I Want For You." I couldn't imagine where it came from; it had to have fallen out of one of the packed boxes, but I didn't remember packing it or even seeing it before. How it appeared on the garage floor with nothing else around it was very bizarre. I couldn't bring myself to read it then. The emotion of the moment prevented any more grief. It would have to wait till later when I was alone or else the movers would have to sweep up pieces of my heart. Was he there with me as I was leaving for the last time? Was he telling me it was okay to move on? Was this a God moment?

The movers stopped for a lunch break before bringing the two moving vans holding my life's treasures. It gave me time to open up the new house, grab a quick bite to eat and await the chaos that would arrive thirty minutes later. Unloading the trucks was faster than loading, and I spent the next three hours directing traffic. Thank goodness I had labeled the forty boxes and where to put them. It was an exhausting day, and when they were finished, there were so many boxes in every room along with the furniture, it was almost impossible to move around. I couldn't help but think that this was the first house I had ever bought on my own; he would never be here to share it; he would never contribute to the memories made here. It didn't feel right, but I knew it was. *God,* I thought, *please help me with these conflicting emotions.*

As the movers left and wished me well in my new home, I stood on the front porch and out of the corner of my eye I was aware of some movement by the huge Maple tree. To my amazement, there hovered a hummingbird, the only one I had seen since the three days following his death. There wasn't even an enticing flower nearby. Had my husband followed me here, letting me know he was still with me? I wanted so badly to believe that.

Before I turned out the light for the night, I remembered the letter on the garage floor. My heart began beating faster as I opened it. In it he had made a list and enumerated all the thoughts he had about me, about us as a couple and what he wanted for us in our new home. It was very sweet, very heartfelt, and though I honestly didn't remember reading it thirty-one years ago, I did remember well this time in our marriage when we made the difficult decision to move. After reading the letter several times, I folded it up and put it away.

Sleep did not come easily that first night in my new bedroom, not because it wasn't comfortable but because my exhaustion gave way to horrible feet and leg cramps and muscle spasms from being on my feet all day. Every time I moved to change positions a new cramp grabbed me until I was afraid to move at all. I knew I had been very hard on my whole body for months; I hurt everywhere. I had been thirty-one years younger the last time we moved, and then there were two of us doing the work. My arthritic hands throbbed from weeks of carrying heavy boxes; my shoulders burned, and now there were the leg and feet cramps. It was painfully obvious I had overdone it, and my tired body was finally getting even.

Why is it we think we can do more than we probably should? As I lay awake, the thought occurred to me that in his last years, his motor functions deteriorated terribly, from walking unassisted to using a cane, to needing a walker and eventually a wheelchair. How many arguments did we have because he refused to accept that he needed these devices? How many times had he fallen because he left his cane or his walker behind? There were too many to count. My husband's delusions were due to dementia; mine, however, to denial of my age limitations.

Eight hours later I reluctantly crawled out of bed to begin my first full day in my new home. It was a beautiful, sunny, June morning and the start of a new chapter in my life. I almost couldn't believe that the house I was living in was the first house I fell in love with six months earlier, and I was grateful no one else had wanted it. The dog was obviously insecure and followed me everywhere, never letting me out of her sight. Knowing my first breakfast would have to be something easy, I had bought four gooey, sugary apple fritters at the bakery; they had been Paul's favorite. All I needed was some caffeine and arthritis meds, and I would be good to go!

As the coffee brewed, I wondered if the morning newspaper and the mail would find me at my new address. I took my second cup of coffee and the newspaper which did find me to the inviting screen porch, one of the spaces that had endeared me to this house from the beginning. The rotating blades of the ceiling fan, the wind chimes I had hung outside earlier, the nearby cooing of some doves and all the luscious sounds of an early summer morning began to ease some of the tension in my body. Though I hated to go inside, dozens of boxes were waiting to be unpacked, and duty called.

I was anticipating the arrival of the phone company to set up my internet, phone and TV's, so I began making a path through the biggest boxes. They were filled with the dining room china, crystal and collectible knick-knacks for the curio cabinet. I loved all these beautiful things: cut crystal from Germany, Limoges porcelain from France, delicate ballerinas from Dresden, Germany, Swarovski crystal from St. Petersburg, Russia, the Provençale village houses bought over the course of our many travels to the south of France, these were things I treasured, and they all made it unbroken to their new home!

After getting through just the first box, I found a path to the front door and welcomed the cable guy. He worked non-stop from 8:00 A.M. until 2:00 P.M. while I continued emptying boxes. Finally, I had phone service, WIFI and TV, and life began feeling a little more normal. I had been living with deadlines for so many months, but now I had none. None of those boxes had a deadline to be opened, and the sudden sense of relief actually made me laugh out loud.

My eighteen year old granddaughter called and asked to come over to practice the piano, entertaining me while I worked. Slowly but surely, I was seeing more empty floor space instead of cardboard and bubble wrap. When she finished we took a cup of coffee out to the porch and enjoyed some teenage conversation. Thank God for a reason to take a break and sit down. Then the doorbell rang; there was my other daughter and her three children. Joy filled me as I watched them go from room to room, especially when they saw the "butterfly room" looking exactly as it had been decorated in the other house. Maybe they would learn to love it here after all. That evening, I spent more time on my back porch and watched an amazing sunset. Wine in hand, I phoned a good friend and realized that now I would have time to reestablish contacts with my friends. The 24/7 caregiving had done a good job of limiting those times. I traded a night of TV for the twilight setting in, tree frogs beginning their nightly songs and lightning bugs illuminating the two huge Pin Oak trees in my yard. This was going to be my nightly ritual, and I had a profound moment of peace. I also used this quiet time to talk to my husband, telling him everything I loved about this space and how much I missed him and wished he could enjoy it with me.

After my first restful night sleep in my new home, which I named *Chez Mémé*, the dog and I repeated our morning ritual on the porch followed by our first walk in the neighborhood and....more boxes. This was going to be an important day since at 3:00 I had to meet my realtor son at the bank for the closing of my old house. It had been five weeks since I had accepted the offer from this buyer, the family with five children. They had made a low bid and we countered; they came up and we came down, and even though the final offer was less than I had hoped, I accepted it. I remembered when we had bought this house so long ago we also made a low offer. Another family made an offer higher than ours, but the seller accepted ours because, I learned later, they really liked my husband. But then, everybody did. So I thought it appropriate to pay it forward and accept a lower bid. Besides, I really wanted my house to be filled with the sounds of happy children. My son had been worried that giving them five weeks before closing could backfire, possibly giving them too much time to have a change of heart. His concern was contagious, and I worried about that, too. They had requested a second walk through before the closing at 10:00A.M. hours before the closing at 3:00. At 10:30 the phone rang and my heart nearly stopped when I saw it was my son calling.

"Did everything go okay?" I asked him, praying for no bad news.

"Well, yes, there was an issue, but I took care of it," he answered tentatively.

"What issue? Everything was fine during their first walk

through and when I left two days ago," I said, trying to keep the panic out of my voice.

"They turned on the garbage disposal, and water gushed out under the sink, but it's okay. I said I took care of it."

"How in the world did you take care of it? I asked, my voice getting louder.

"I bought them a $200.00 gift card to Home Depot to replace it. Problem solved. It's all good," he said calmly. "See you at 3:00." I nearly collapsed in a chair with relief.

It wasn't hard to keep busy until it was time to leave. My little insecure dog would have to be left alone in the house for the first time. Somehow, she sensed my approaching departure. I felt sorry for her, all her familiar spaces and routines had been upended, and now I wouldn't be here to follow around. But I had no choice. I had a house to sell!

How anticlimactic the process was. The buyers were so excited about their new house. I couldn't help but recall having the same feeling on the day we bought it thirty-one years ago. I was pleased to see their joy. The youngest of their five children, a six month old son, was with them.

"And so what room is going to be yours, little man?" I asked. Mom replied that he was going to get our youngest daughter's room which they were going to paint blue. For a split second it stung to imagine how her pretty peach colored room would look for a little boy.

The closing was finished in a half hour. Just thirty minutes later, I no longer owned two houses. I shook the buyers' hands and wished them many happy years in the house where Paul and I had created so many memories. With a lump in my throat and a fat check in my hands, I went to the bank and deposited it, but not before stopping to buy a bottle of Scotch to celebrate later!

After a peaceful Happy Hour and a healthy dinner of chicken and Cobb salad, I turned on a CD of Andrew Lloyd Weber's music, lit a scented candle and sat on my porch to welcome another sunset. Dusk was almost mesmerizing as darkness crept in and fireflies appeared. The dog, always sitting next to me, was on high alert to every sound, every passing car and every barking dog in the distance. Every noise caught her attention as she looked in the direction from where it came. The darker it got, the more I found myself on high alert as well, as much as that is possible while sipping a second cocktail. Suddenly, her little body tensed, and she ran out into the backyard, barking the angry bark that always meant a dog was walking outside her house. She tore out to the back fence; I could see nothing in the dark to trigger this response from her, so I followed her outside. Just then the big, white-tailed deer slowly came into focus, strutted the entire length of the fence, then stood there like a statue and stared at me. My fearless, great white hunter was back on duty protecting me. She would be fine, I knew, and suddenly I was filled with intense gratitude for this day and this night. This house, this porch, this beautiful yard and God's creatures attracted to it, this new chapter was beginning to feel very right.

The following day, my granddaughter requested more piano time. I would always make time for her, precious moments to share before she went off to college, time that forced me to take a break. It was June 30th, and the heat index was climbing to record breaking temperatures and humidity for this early in the summer. It was the kind of weather too dangerous last year for my husband; congestive heart failure and asthma made it too difficult for him to breathe. He had died just days after a heat spell like this one had sapped the little energy he had left by that time. I wondered how long it would take for me to discontinue these kinds of memories and comparisons, these moments that would continue to take my thoughts back to him.

When she left, I put on the Andrew Lloyd Weber CD again. A song from Phantom of the Opera began, and for the first time the lyrics screamed at me. *"Wish somehow you could be here again......Wish that I could hear your voice again."* Suddenly, my throat tightened, my eyes filled and overflowed, and I felt like I couldn't catch a breath. It wasn't due to the heat but to the honesty of those words searing themselves into my soul. There was no way to stop the emotion of the moment. I couldn't have stopped even if I had tried. I sobbed once again for the loss of him, the loss of his goofy, corny sense of humor, the loss of his awful singing voice, the loss of his love. All I could do was say his name over and over.

There had been other such unanticipated moments of grief over the last year, moments that came with absolutely no warning, but this was the most intense one in quite a while. I turned off the music; this was an emotional trigger I had no time for with so much work to do. My office was still calling me to get rid of boxes so I could find more floor space and make my way to my desk. I dried my eyes, blew my nose, and filled a few more tissues until seven more boxes were gone. Finally I could get to my desk and the bills due to be paid the next day.

Months before, I had put all my office furniture in storage so the room could be painted and get a new carpet. I hadn't gone through the drawers since then. When I got to the last drawer, way in the back was a stack of old greeting cards from Paul that I had saved over the years. They were old Valentines, some dated, some not, some signed with legible signatures from before the Parkinson's disease had robbed him of readable handwriting. I opened each one and read it remembering how important Valentine's Day had always been to us. Finally there was only one left, and I gasped when I opened it. It was a card I honestly didn't remember receiving, there was no date; there was no signature. But it was a card that had allowed him to record his message to me. There was his voice. "Happy Valentine's Day, Dee. I love you, and I hope we have many more." I played it over and over; it was more comforting than sad. How great was this God moment, for unlike the song lyrics, I could hear his voice again!

-Three-

PEACE

Just one more month and he would have been gone for a year. I could hardly wrap my head around that fact; it seemed at times that I hadn't seen him for years and other times like yesterday. As well as selling my house, finding a house and moving in, there were two other projects that had occupied my time during the first year of widowhood. The journal I had been writing for the last three years of his life was finally about to be published as well as another historic fiction chapter book for children, the third in the series. The journal became the book *In Sickness and in Health. A Wife/ Caregiver Reflects on the Words "Before I Do"*. It had been one of the most important projects I had ever worked on, and I was very proud of it. I had no idea if it was marketable or if anyone else would find it worth reading. Actually, that didn't even matter to me at the time. I dedicated it to the Hospice nurses who had helped us for over two years, and I couldn't wait to surprise each of them with a copy.

July came in, as it always does, like a fiery furnace, and I was still looking at boxes everywhere. Little by little the rooms began coming together and looking like home. I began loving this space even more than when I had first seen it. All the updates made a huge difference, and my children decided it wasn't a bad idea to buy it after all! On the first night to put out the garbage, I was struggling with about twenty large, collapsed cardboard boxes, trying to carry more than I should have to the curb. My neighbor was doing the same. He saw me or maybe heard me grunt in pain. He came over and asked if I needed help and then he introduced himself. He was the first neighbor to do that, and I was most appreciative. The neighbors, at least in the houses closest to mine, seemed very friendly, and whenever I took the dog for a walk, I met a few more. I knew I had made the right move choosing this place. The gorgeous, extensive gardens in the photos online were anything but gorgeous after the house had been vacant for two years. The weeds were definitely winning, so much so that I wasn't sure what was a weed and what wasn't. Since my sister is a Master Gardener, I had to solicit her help. She cleared out so much debris, I couldn't believe it. But I was beginning to see the potential in restoring these gardens to their original glory. It would be a work in progress for years, but that was okay. Planning was half the fun.

The fourth of July provided a huge surprise. I had always loved fireworks and had missed being able to see them for so many years. The last Fourth of July of Paul's life I gave into a pity party when I had to put my husband to bed and heard the fireworks in the distance but couldn't get to see any. Of course I didn't realize at that moment he wouldn't live to see the end of the month. Now the holiday was here again and the sounds of the fireworks were deafening, so close to home! The dog ran for cover, and I went out on my back deck to have a look. Somewhere nearby, someone was putting on a nearly commercial grade display of fireworks that exploded in all their glory right over my back yard. It was so close, in fact, that I got a bit nervous as I watched hot embers floating towards my roof! What an amazing sight it was and I had to smile wondering if my husband had arranged it for my pleasure.

The first anniversary of his death was upon me at the end of July, and I wasn't sure how I felt about it. I had managed to keep myself so incredibly busy all year that the moments of emotional breakdown were infrequent. I was taking pride in the fact that I thought I was doing really well emotionally. The Hospice group had sent me a pamphlet with a check list to do a self-assessment of how I was dealing with my grief after a year. I read it with great interest and once again, pat myself on the back for a job well done. Then I went to his anniversary Mass at church and happened to see the parish nurse who had come to the house with the priest to administer the Sacrament of the Sick as he lay dying. She greeted me with open arms and asked me how I was doing. The words, "Pretty well" stuck in my throat, and the tears began to run down my cheeks taking me by surprise and destroying the moment. When I could collect myself I said, "Well, at least I thought I was doing well, better than this." She just smiled and said she understood. Had I just been running around like a crazy person for the year and shoving the grief aside?

Coincidentally, (or are there really any coincidences,) the publisher launched the memoir the same week as Paul's first anniversary. It was really a beautiful book, and I read it cover to cover again. It was 216 pages of gut wrenching honesty, and when I read it, I couldn't believe all we had been through together. It was actually a blessing to be able to re-live it all, because when I closed the book, I said aloud, "Whew! I am so relieved for both of us that you are not suffering any longer and I am not so stressed." It was an eye opening moment and one I needed.

The time had come to invite my Hospice friends to dinner to show off my new house and surprise them with their copies of the book. The head nurse, Tracy, who had become a very good friend, had tears in her eyes when she read the dedication to them. They were both totally shocked and most grateful, and I was very pleased to have been able to acknowledge how vitally important they had been in our lives. It was a wonderful candlelit evening of pizza and wine on the screen porch and good conversation with the two women who had spent so much time with my husband and had helped me to survive the most difficult time in my entire life. We found ourselves talking about him most of the evening, laughing at some of the lighter moments they had spent with him, and it felt so good to remember him in an upbeat manner. That hadn't happened in forever! When they left, my good friend turned to me and said the perfect words I needed to hear. "I sense a real peace in this house, and I am so happy for you." I cleaned up the kitchen, poured another glass of wine and went out to the porch again. With the candles still flickering and the fireflies creating Christmas trees in July, I had a heartfelt talk with my dear husband, and I truly felt that he was still there with me.

-Four-

NEW FIRSTS

There is one word in the English language which I have come to hate; the word is "widow". I know that sounds ridiculous, but for me it has always conjured up images that are less than pleasant. Even all 176 references to this word in Scripture make her sound like a pathetic, old woman who is totally helpless, dependent on charity for survival, at risk of being robbed blind and lumped with the poor orphans. I remember the moment after Paul died when I had to acknowledge this word for the first time. I was checking in to a medical appointment and filling out all the required pages of information that seem to go on forever. I came to the line requiring marital status. There were my choices: single, married, divorced, widowed. How many scores of times had I circled "married" and almost did again out of habit until I realized that I would not be circling that word ever again in my life. I saw "widow" as the last of the choices, and I felt the lump in my throat. The word stared back at me, the last choice, the end of the line. It was like it was describing my life. Was I at the end of the line? Did I really have to circle the one word that seemed like the least desirable word in the list? The answer was yes! I felt hot all over, felt my heart beating harder through my shirt and tears began welling up in my eyes, and I wanted to throw the papers back at the registrar and run out of the room. How many more times would I have to acknowledge this new reality before it would not feel like a slap in the face? I turned in the forms after collecting myself, and just when I felt more in control again, she asked me without looking up from her desk, "And is Paul still the best contact person?" I choked back more tears as I tried to get out my response. "I wish he was, but he died recently." I guess I shocked her with the tone of my voice, and when she finally looked up and saw the tears rolling down my face, she added quickly, "Oh, I am so sorry." She hesitated uncomfortably before asking, "Whose name would you like me to list instead?" At that moment, I didn't care if I gave her the dog's name; if it couldn't be Paul's, I really didn't care.

By the time I got home, I had replayed this mini drama in my head over and over. I had a new status in life, one I would never have chosen for myself, but there it was, not to be denied. Was I really, like that word, at the end of the line? Was I totally dependent and helpless? Was I a pathetic, old woman as the widow is depicted in every biblical reference? Surely not, but I was the only person who could negate all those stereotypes. I may have been at the end of the line in the world of romance; I couldn't imagine ever marrying a second time for reasons too many to list. The accomplishments of the past year certainly proved I had not been helpless. Yes, I was dependent on my son, son-in-law and daughters to get me through the craziness of relocating, but I was not dependent on anyone else. Yes, there were moments when I felt pathetic, as I recalled my emotion in the doctor's office earlier, but I survived. And old? Well, I realized I was now of *une certaine age*, as the French so delicately put it, but I didn't feel old. I may not have liked my widowhood, but I had to make it the best it could be. I recalled the pamphlet the Hospice group had sent me at the end of the first year. It had warned of the possibility that the second year could be harder than the first. Oh great! That's a pleasant thought, I said out loud. Not if I can help it! But where to begin? It was August, and the house had come together nicely. I had no more big domestic projects to do. I remembered that my kids had said they had been worried that when the dust finally settled I might fall apart. So I decided at that very moment to make sure they wouldn't have to pick up pieces of me all over the dusty floor. Fortunately, my French class for retirees at the university was going to begin shortly, and there were eight weeks of preparation to get organized. It was a good place to start. I was also anxious to get back into the world of socializing with my girlfriends who had been so supportive during my years of caregiving. It was time to invite them over for coffee, show them my house, or go out to lunch and get caught up. I made sure to schedule a date every week. And all of them wanted to buy a copy of my book. That was an added bonus I hadn't seen coming. One of my oldest friends from childhood was experiencing the beginnings of caregiving for her husband who had been recently diagnosed with Parkinson's. She bought four copies of my book, one for herself and one for each of her children! Every copy I sold lifted me up a bit more.

Before my husband and I had to stop traveling, we had seen more of the world than most people ever see in their lifetime. After his diagnosis, we made travel a priority knowing there would surely come a time when it would be too difficult. There were several international voyages left undone from our bucket list, but the thought of doing them alone really didn't sound like fun. But I had also loved travel, and I did miss it. I had to admit I was just too afraid to do it alone. But then something happened to encourage me to get the suitcases out again.

Paul's Irish twin brother who was just eleven months younger and his wife, who was like another sister to me, lived in Colorado. We had spent a wonderful time with them eight years earlier in Rocky Mountain National Park when we were celebrating my husband's 70th birthday. Knowing what nature lovers we both were, they wanted us to time the visit during the Elk rutting season in mid-September, a phenomenon that was truly amazing, they said. Another one of Paul's brothers and his sister joined us in Colorado for a family reunion birthday surprise, and every photo showed him looking happier than I had seen him in years. September was right around the corner, and they invited me to come back to see the Elk again. This time I would be alone. To make the invitation even more tempting, their daughter, who taught fourth grade in Denver, had been using two of my children's books as read-alouds in class for years. She invited me to come and treat her students to an author visit and hold a pre-sale of the books. This was just too good to pass up. I really wanted to go, but then the fear gene kicked in. Paul had always been in charge of all things related to airports, and I was terrified to tackle this alone for the first time. Immediately, I felt like the pathetic, dependent widow, needing someone to hold my hand and take the lead. *Snap out of it,* I thought. *You've been in airports all over the world. It's only Denver, and you'll be meeting family! Get a grip!* And so I accepted the invitation.

After making one wrong turn in the airport since lots had changed since I was there last, I found my gate and waited for boarding. To make life easier, I had managed to pack a large, heavy satchel type purse and just one very heavy carry-on bag so as not to run the risk of lost luggage. Finally, it was time to board, and I was quite proud of myself for getting this far on my own. But moments later another pathetic moment occurred when I couldn't lift my heavy bag into the overhead compartment. Fortunately, a young, muscular guy took pity and did it for me.My pride being sufficiently checked, I settled in to my seat and prepared for take-off. Then another mini moment of sad, self-awareness occurred. Every flight Paul and I had ever taken made me nervous. I hated take-offs and landings, and it was our habit to hold hands through each one. Usually mine was white-knuckled until we were safely up or down. We were finally prepared to go, engines roaring as we taxied down the runway. I instinctively went to reach for his hand and remembered just in time to not grab the hand of the stranger next to me. Instead, I held my own hand, closed my eyes and pretended it was his. Having done the same thing upon landing in Denver, I had to ask the strapping young man who had helped me with my luggage to get it down again. I discovered that people are very nice to single women of *une certaine age.*

Another moment of panic on my first solo voyage was not far

behind. I had been eight years younger when we were last there, and the altitude hit me as soon as I was in the airport. Maybe it was because I was pulling one heavy carry-on and shouldering another very heavy purse, but I was breathless before I got too far. To make matters worse, my sister-in-law had given me rather sketchy directions as to where to find her, and this airport was like a city it was so big. *Well,* I thought, *I had always told my high school French students there was no such thing as a stupid question, so all I have to do is ask someone how to get from point A to point B.* And *Voila!* Another very nice agent came to rescue the single lady of *une certaine age*.

And there she was! My sister-in-law was truly a sight for sore eyes. I could have cried knowing I wouldn't have to find my way around alone for the next week. Yes, I would be dependent on family for the next few days, but that didn't feel like such a bad thing after all. We went to our hotel for the night and then met her daughter who invited us to her home for dinner. I hadn't seen her, her husband and two children for eight years, and it was a joyous reunion. She had pre-ordered the books the children bought, enough of them to pay for my flight, and I spent at least an hour signing each one before going to school with her the following morning. There isn't anything more enjoyable to me than being in a classroom with children and sharing what I know with them. These were really bright kids who asked great questions about cave-art, the subject of the book they had read together. Every question I asked them they answered with enthusiasm as fifteen or twenty hands shot up in the air, begging to be called on. There was one little boy I could have adopted and taken home he was so cute. He was over-the-top excited about the subject and wanted to answer every question himself. It was obvious the children in the two classes with whom I had met had loved the book, and I was overjoyed. It was a great beginning to my first solo trip, and I hadn't even seen or heard an elk yet!

When I slipped from teacher mode back into family mode, my sister-in-law and I made the trip via light rail from Denver to Longmont where she lived. It was an enjoyable, but long day of travel, and I couldn't wait to get rid of the heavy bags, take off my shoes and relax. She and her husband had also gotten eight years older, and we slipped into an easy rhythm of activity. But there would continue to be a few difficult and emotional moments yet to experience.

For years she had been a guitarist who played and sang at Mass, and as a volunteer, she visited nursing homes to play the music for their services. The following day, we visited one of her groups. As luck would have it, this was a service where an elderly man was receiving his commission to be a distributer of the Eucharist. I was doing just fine until this ceremony began. But once it did, my mind immediately traveled back to my former family room as the distributer came to our house and brought Communion to Paul in his recliner chair, since I never took him to church during flu season. Once again the pathetic widow couldn't stop the tears and there was nothing I could do. I hadn't seen this coming, and I was completely embarrassed. It didn't help that I had not one tissue in my purse and the sniffing was ridiculous. I apologized to my sister-in-law and tried to explain on the way home what had triggered my drama. She had one more service later in the day, and I told her I had better take a pass and stay home.

I couldn't wait to leave the following day for the cabin in Estes Park, right outside the National Park. It was a glorious day and soon the majesty of the mountains came into view. We had packed a picnic for lunch, and before we arrived at the picnic grounds, we saw our first elk, a young female grazing by the side of the road. I still think they are some of God's most beautiful creatures. We drove around looking for a table, and my heart was once again in my throat when we pulled into the exact same spot where the four of us had lunched eight years ago. It was a gorgeous spot, a brook bubbling close by, Stellar Jays waiting for food to drop. It was exactly as I had remembered it, even the fallen log where I had sat with Paul by the brook was still there. I had to walk away for a moment and collect myself again so as not to spoil a beautiful picnic. I was afraid this trip might have been a mistake after all. I hoped I was wrong.

We arrived shortly after lunch at our log cabin high up in the mountains. It was an incredible setting at 8000 feet that he would have loved, but I couldn't allow myself to think about that too long. The mountains had always been the place where he had found his peace; for me it was always the ocean. As we began unloading the car, ten wild turkeys meandered by welcoming us to our home for the next three days. You could hear the wind singing in the pine trees and in the distance as dusk fell, the unmistakable sounds of bugling elk were echoing through the mountainside. Yes, I missed my travel partner, but I also felt he was there with me and happy that I had had the courage to make the trip.

It really was a magical time with more elk than we had even seen the last time. The bulls put on quite a show for their ladies, sometimes up close and personal to the tourists. There were so many photo ops everywhere! I couldn't have been any more excited if I had been ten years old. But the time to leave came way too soon, and as we were driving back at their house, an overwhelming sadness engulfed me. After unloading the car they went to take their daily afternoon naps, and I went out on their deck and gave in to a good cry. But the thing was I didn't know why I was so sad. After mulling this over for a while, I realized what it was.

For the last few days, I had watched the two of them laugh together, talk together, share everything together. It had been so long since Paul and I had enjoyed moments like these, and the realization that I was going home to an empty house with no one to talk to but the dog felt terrible. In that moment, I didn't know how to talk myself out of this pathetic funk. And it scared me. But God came to my rescue, as He always seems to do.

I was sitting in the Denver airport after a tearful farewell to my hosts the following day. An announcement came over the intercom that the flight was going to be delayed for two hours! *Oh wonderful,* I thought. *How will I fill this time?* I took out my journal and updated it; that took twenty minutes. I grabbed a bite to eat; that took another thirty minutes. I got out my phone and began checking for emails and what the latest thought provoking information was on Facebook. There I found a posting by a parent of one of my former high school students. She had also been widowed, and this post was an extensive list of all the good things about living alone! I almost laughed out loud while I was reading it. It was good stuff, and the significance of the timing was impossible to ignore.

I boarded the plane, got help with my bags, held my own hands again at take-off and settled in for the flight home to my little dog who greeted me with all the unconditional love only a dog can give. I could check off another "first" in my life as a widow, and it was all good.

-Five-

JUST ME

So here I was in the third month of my second year in this new chapter of my life. I was relieved to have weathered all the dreaded firsts after a loved one dies; the first Thanksgiving was hard but made easier when my son offered to host it for the first time in his life, and I was grateful. The first Christmas was equally difficult, but the entire family got through it with grace, and I was grateful for all their efforts. The first New Year's Eve was awful with no one to kiss except the dog as the ball came down. The first Valentine's Day was really tough for reasons already mentioned, but I did replay that audio card a few times, and it helped. Then there were other days like the first Father's Day and the first birthday after he was gone and finally the first anniversary of his death. All those firsts were predictable, and we can try to prepare for them as best we can and say thank you when they are finished. But there are also those unpredictable firsts like circling the word "widow" on a medical form or taking a vacation alone. How many more would there be?

I hadn't given much thought over the last year to the fact that I was no longer part of a couple. Paul and I had been a couple for five years of dating and fifty years of marriage. We never had a huge number of couples friends, and a few of those we did have had dropped by the wayside when life got rough. Gratefully, there were three who stayed with us through thick and thin until the end. Funny how you can judge true friendship when life isn't fun any longer. It's pretty eye opening. For fifty-five years we were referred to as Paul and Dee until it was like one word, "paulandee."

The first time I felt the effects of this was at a function with family on Veterans Day four months after he died. I was invited to join my sister, brother-in-law, his brother and wife and my niece and her husband at a special Mass followed by lunch at my niece's home. I was looking forward to this event especially since I hadn't seen her new home yet, and the Mass would be very moving. This is a family group I had spent countless hours with over the years, and I was always comfortable with them, however it is also a group of people who are very loquacious, and it can be hard to get a word in. But I was used to that. The conversation flowed predictably during lunch, and as the afternoon progressed I felt the first tugs of depression setting in, a feeling that made me want to exit the premises immediately. And just like on my brother-in-law's deck in Colorado, I didn't know what set it off. Given this cloud settling over me, I was grateful to not have to add much to the conversation. On the drive home, the self-analysis began once again until I figured it out. And there it was. This was the first social event I had attended where I was number seven in a group which used to be eight. I was the only person not part of a couple. It was like a sucker punch to my soul when I realized this. From that point on, it would always be "just me" instead of Paul and me.

The three loyal "couples friends" had been very dear to us. Two of the men had been colleagues of Paul's. We had season tickets to the ballet with one couple for decades. The other had invited us to their vacation home in Hilton Head, South Carolina several times. The third couple was our next door neighbor with whom we had spent many hours over the years, going out to dinner, having ice cream on their patio, traveling to a Notre Dame game in South Bend, Indiana and playing board games in the kitchen. We even exchanged Christmas gifts every year. All three of these couples came to Paul's seventy-fifth birthday party and also to our fiftieth anniversary party. I found myself wondering how things would be now that it was "just me." Those two words hit me almost as hard as the word "widow". From now on it would always be just me. Why hadn't I seen this coming? It was never listed in the pamphlets on what to expect with grieving. Why didn't someone fill me in on this? The couple with whom we went to the ballet had been most accommodating during the last dance season by changing their seats to be with us in the handicapped section where I could push Paul in the wheelchair. They even agreed to go to the matinee performances instead of the Saturday night shows since Paul couldn't stay up that late any longer. I wanted to continue to buy two tickets for each ballet and had planned to take my daughters or granddaughters with me to fill the seat Paul had occupied.

The first season opener came just two months after his death, and our friends had a conflict with travel and offered me their two tickets. I gratefully accepted and suggested that instead of putting the tickets in the mail, they come to see my new house and have a pizza party on the porch. We had a wonderful evening for the first time even though it was "just me". The conversation flowed effortlessly all evening as did the wine, and I felt an interesting change in the group dynamic. And it was okay.

The second couple with whom we had been close friends since our children were toddlers also continued to make an effort to spend time with "just me" and eventually they even invited me to come to Hilton Head again by myself. I felt incredibly blessed to still have all four of them in my life and honestly surprised and relieved that they still welcomed time with me alone. I wasn't sure how I would feel going to Hilton Head alone, but I filed that suggestion away.

Our former neighbors were going through their own difficulties with her health, but they still managed to visit me in my new home a couple of times. She had multiple health issues and was struggling day to day just to get around. It was at Paul's 75th birthday party that she had tearfully shared with me that she had been recently diagnosed with breast cancer. Then the radiation had damaged her heart tissue and created another problem. Her husband had taken on the role of 24/7 caregiver, and we talked occasionally about the fears that accompanied that job. When she would be in the hospital, I took him some dinners. After I moved I tried to phone once a week so I could keep tabs on how she was doing. And it was never good. I watched him lose weight as I had done in the months before Paul died, and I always worried about him, too. Another former neighbor would call me whenever they had to call 911 for her, so I was always in the loop. He never called me, but that was alright. Then right before the second anniversary of Paul's death I received a phone call from him at 8:15 in the morning to tell me she had died during the night. I was devastated and told him I would come over later that day.

I knew there were no words adequate to say at that moment, and there really wasn't a need for them. So I just listened as he cried and told me how much he "loved that girl'. My heart broke for him, and we cried together unashamedly; he knew I understood all too well the agony of that moment. He told me later that he hated this new station in his life. I saw him at Mass every Sunday, and we spoke briefly before Mass started. I told him, in a joking way, that it would help him if he would call his friends sometime, specifically me. He said he would, but I wasn't holding my breath. After six weeks, he did invite himself over for coffee after dropping off his grandson at pre-school. I was so surprised and pleased that he decided he would be comfortable being with "just me", and we talked for three hours. He was in that phase when he needed to talk about her with somebody who knew all they had been through. I was more than happy to be that somebody. When he had to leave he said, "Well, this was most enjoyable. I'll do it again sometime." So I joked with him. "Well, you know when I was a teenager my mother always said that girls don't ever call boys. So if you want to do this again, you'll have to call me!" He laughed, said that was bull, gave me a hug and left.

After the Veterans Day Mass, the holidays were just around the corner, and I was almost giddy figuring out how to decorate my new house. I hadn't felt much like doing this the first Christmas season after Paul died, but now I had new rooms to decorate, and I was up for the challenge. It was a real revelation to me when I recognized that I needed to continue this activity not for anyone else but for just me. I loved seeing each room transform into a Christmas wonderland, and I couldn't wait to put up all three Christmas trees just like I had always done in the old house. I had already put one of them up during the summer. It was our travel tree holding dozens of ornaments we had amassed over our decades of travel. They came from all over the world, and in the latter years of Paul's life, we would do it together. He would choose an ornament, and I would ask him to remember something about that place. It had been an easy way to challenge his failing memory for as long as I could. The first Christmas after he died, I couldn't put it up; it was just too hard. But I decided that when I moved, it was going to stand on the back porch year 'round so I could relive those wonderful vacations any time I wanted.

The second tree was the Grandchildren tree, and probably my favorite. It was an old artificial tree that had belonged to my parents, it was showing signs of old age and not too great to look at, but when the eight children came over Thanksgiving weekend every year to decorate it with ornaments depicting every Disney character ever created, ornaments from TV shows like the Brady Bunch and board games like their favorite one, Sorry, ornaments from Star Wars with Darth Vader breathing audibly when you walked past the tree, it was a joyful sight to see. Every year I bought each one of the kids a new ornament to add, and I couldn't even begin to estimate the dollar value of all those ornaments. For a straggly tree, it was probably worth more than the other two combined. For the first Grandchildren Tree event in the new house, I decided that since there really wasn't any more room on the tree for new ornaments, and since they were all getting older, we would begin a new tradition. All the ornaments, nearly 150 of them, were displayed on a table in the new rec room. Before decorating could begin, they each could choose a favorite ornament to take home with them for their own Christmas trees. I had them grouped by category; fairy princesses in one pile, movie characters in another, TV characters like all the different Muppets in another pile and so on. I gave them a chance to walk all around the table and try to decide their choice. It was so much fun watching them make a decision, then change their mind and choose another they liked even more. Honestly it took longer for this activity than it did to decorate the entire tree. And I have to admit that there were several ornaments I loved so much I was praying that no one would choose them! When it was a *fait accompli*, their parents came for Happy Hour to admire the kids' handiwork. This had been a really good first!

The third tree was the big family tree that had always been in the living room. It was a seven foot Blue Spruce that had graced our home for all thirty-one Christmases. It was so big I wasn't sure it would fit in my new family room, but thankfully, it did. I decided to put it up the day after Thanksgiving. It took most of the day just to assemble it, shaping each branch and each stem. I figured I would do the lights and the ornaments later, but I wanted to at least get the angel on top. I always needed a step ladder to do this, and it usually required several attempts to finally look right. The family room was one step down from the kitchen, and the tree stood in the corner where the two rooms converged. I thought it would be smart to position the ladder in the kitchen so I wouldn't have to stretch as far. But when I did, the front legs of the ladder went over the step into the tree and I flew backwards on to the hardwood kitchen floor, landing smack on my tailbone. There are no words to describe the terror of that moment, the incredible pain, the fear I had broken a hip. But oddly enough, my first thought was, "*Please, God, don't let my son be right that I should have bought a ranch instead of a two story!*" I lay there for a moment almost afraid to move. Everything hurt including my back, my tailbone, and my head which had cracked against a small cabinet. Eventually, I got the courage to move slowly on to all fours and determined that nothing was broken. I knew it could have been so much worse, but for that moment the reality of there being "just me" in that house was a bit frightening. Earlier in the week I had gone to the liquor store to stock up for the holiday entertaining. Unfortunately, I tripped up the curb in front of multiple passing cars and landed hard on my hands and knees. Thankfully, nothing was injured too badly except my pride. Bur after falling off the ladder, I spent the next few weeks sitting on an ice bag and most grateful for the liquor purchased after I fell up the curb!

-Six-
ALONE VS. LONELY

It's intriguing, I think, that embarking upon widowhood has made certain words and phrases resonate louder in my head, like the word "widow" and the expression "just me". As a writer, words have always fascinated me, but it never occurred to me that a specific word or expression could take on more than its logical meaning or definition. However, embarking on this next chapter of my life made it abundantly clear that it was indeed possible for logic to go right out the window.

There has always been a huge difference in my mind between the word lonely and the word alone. Webster defines alone as 'without another person' and lonely as 'solitary, unhappy at being alone.' We all know people who seem to need people around them, extroverts psychologists call them, who feed off the interaction with others and are energized by them. Introverts, on the other hand, don't seem to need people quite as much and in fact find socializing at times more exhausting than energizing. I was always one of the latter. As a child, I could entertain myself for hours. I didn't avoid being with other children; I just didn't need to be with anyone to be happy. I spent countless hours listening to records in my room and singing along. I knew the lyrics to every musical that came out in the 50's and 60's. Oklahoma, Carrousel, The King and I, West Side Story, My Fair

Lady...I loved them all. I wrote poetry; I read every Nancy Drew book ever written. I practiced my ballet steps. I composed songs on the piano. This introversion continued into my teen years and adulthood. I never had a gaggle of girlfriends but rather one or two good friends. In retrospect, I never felt the need to work at making friends. It wasn't a priority. I was never lonely.

When I was a young wife and mother, Paul had to travel frequently for his career. It seemed something catastrophic frequently happened during his absence; the dog had to be euthanized; one of the kids got hurt necessitating a run to the ER; it was always something. Soon, like a classical conditioning response, I began to equate being alone with a crisis. I would cry before he left, anticipating the worst and wondering if I'd be able to handle whatever happened all alone. During one of his trips, I asked myself why I reacted like this. It certainly wasn't fair to put him through this drama every time he had to pack a suitcase. I wasn't lonely when he was gone; I was too busy being both mom and dad to be lonely. But I was alone. I remember thinking, *I'm not afraid to grow old; I'm not even afraid to die. But I'm afraid to grow old alone.*

Recognizing that my husband had a family history of heart disease and that he refused to give up smoking a pack of cigarettes a day, the very real possibility of growing old alone was always in the back of my mind. And it scared me to death. I had nightmares about him leaving me alone with a family to raise just like his father had done after a sudden, massive heart attack at age fifty-eight. I think in some ways, in the back of my mind, I was always preparing myself for this inevitable disaster. But he didn't die young thanks to open heart surgery at age fifty-seven, three months before the same age his father had died. He graced me with twenty more years of marriage, and when he did leave this world from congestive heart failure and Parkinson's disease, he left me with three adult children and eight wonderful grandchildren. But he did leave me getting older and...alone.

That first year after he died, I kept myself too busy to be lonely or even to think about being alone. There was just too much to do.

The first night alone in my new home was a blessing; I was too tired to feel lonely. Even after the conclusion of the first year living alone, there had rarely been moments of feeling lonely. But lying on my back on the kitchen floor and staring up at a Christmas tree without an angel on top suddenly made it all too clear what it felt like to be really alone. What if I had broken something? My phone wasn't anywhere close by to call for help. That thought really bothered me after I had finally collected my wits. The grandchildren were coming over two days later to decorate their tree, their parents coming later for Happy Hour. I wasn't sure I was going to tell them what had happened, but when they saw me limping around, I had to tell them the truth. Then my son joked, "So, mom, you fell up the curb in front of the liquor store, and you fell off a ladder in the kitchen. Is it time to get you a Life Alert call button?" Everybody laughed at his levity, everybody but me. My response was, "Well, I know I will never get on a ladder again, so when there is a difficult job to do, I'll just have to ask you to come over and do it for me!" Then I laughed.

A couple of months after the first anniversary, it was time to resume my French conversation class at the university. This was a particularly terrific group of people and a class I enjoyed more than any other in the past. One of the women was an avid traveler, and she and her husband had been all over the world. She knew that Paul and I had shared this passion as well, and she asked me if I had considered getting back into world travel. My immediate response was no, not at all. The thought of going to the places left unvisited on our bucket list all by myself was not very appealing, but she encouraged me to reconsider the idea. To make sure I did, the following week she came to class carrying six catalogs from the company they used for their travel plans, Roads Scholar. I thanked her and told her I would look through them. But instead, when I got home I put them in the closet unexamined. Travel alone? There was that word again. I couldn't imagine ever wanting to go anywhere, especially somewhere Paul had wanted to visit, without him. It was just unthinkable and too painful to imagine. I had tackled traveling alone to Colorado, but that was family and much easier. The catalogs stayed unopened in the closet for three months.

I awoke on a frigid January 1st, ready to take on a new year. As I had always done, I got out my extensive list of resolutions and goals to achieve from the previous year to assess how I had done, what I had accomplished and where I had fallen short. This always drove Paul crazy, and I have to admit that the effort that went into making these lists was amazing. The obsessive list maker in me organized my goals for the year into categories: physical health goals, social goals, home improvement goals, mind improving goals and on and on. Then each of those categories had sub-lists. When that was finished, the last list included strategies to accomplish each of the goals on the other lists! It was always a masterpiece of optimism. I would proudly show it to Paul and ask him what his resolutions were, and he'd respond, "You've got to be kidding." Well, I guess opposites do attract.

Now it was time to make my new lists for the upcoming year. I have to admit they weren't quite as extensive as they once were, but still challenging enough. When I completed the task, I remembered those six catalogs in the closet; they still haunted me, so I decided to just glance through them. It would be something fun to do on a cold, January day. I had been told that this company catered to the single traveler, making sure that no one ever felt excluded. By the time I had finished the first one, I was beginning to feel the first stirrings of excitement. I imagined myself going to one place or another, but then I would always come back to the word 'alone' and the excitement faded. This company did offer fabulous getaways, and I could understand why my friend in class had chosen them.

In 2007, Paul and I took what we called the trip of our lifetime. It started in Santiago, Chili, continued south cruising through the Chilean fjords, crossing the dreaded Drake Passage, the roughest waters ever on a good day, because it is where the Atlantic and Pacific come together, then cruising to the outer islands of Antarctica before cruising back north through the Drake Passage to Patagonia on the tip of Argentina and finishing in Buenos Aries. Our initial crossing of the Drake Passage was interesting since we encountered a bad storm through already rough waters. Most of the crew and the passengers were sick, but somehow we did well. We saw thousands of Penguins and learned so much from the naturalists on board. My sister even took a photo of me squatting down with one little cutie and talking to him. She sent it in to the travel company and it appeared in the next catalog! We received certificates verifying that we had set foot on the continent of Antarctica, and Paul said, "Now we have to go to The Arctic." But we never made it before he couldn't travel.

As I was leafing through the catalogs, there was an itinerary that began in the Canadian Arctic and cruised south through the Baffin Islands and Greenland. It was a nature packed excursion very similar to the kind we had experienced in Antarctica. I turned down the corner of the page and moved on with my browsing but kept going back to the Arctic. How Paul would have loved this experience! Maybe if I began to travel again I could start with this one for him. I couldn't get it out of my mind for days afterwards and finally decided that I would never know if traveling alone was something I could enjoy if I didn't do it once. And what better way to start than to choose an itinerary that would probably be breathtaking. I figured if I hated the experience, I'd never have to do it again. So I called the company to get more information.

I told them I was a single traveler, and the first thing they asked was whether I wanted them to match me up with another single to share a state room. I said no to that since it would defeat the purpose. There were no single cabins left for that travel season, but he said I could sign up for the same trip for the following year and be the first to get a single room. There were only twenty-four passengers permitted on this voyage so being alone would not be so intimidating. I decided to take the plunge, sign on the dotted line and put down a deposit before I had a chance to change my mind. When I hung up the phone, I said out loud "Oh, God, what have I done? I was thirteen years younger in Antarctica than I would be in the Arctic!"

Secretly, I was proud of myself for having the courage to take this first step, but also scared to death. Could I really do this alone? I figured if I changed my mind later, I would just lose the deposit, and that would be okay. But I also knew very well that I would be disappointed in myself for not going through with it. The departure date was eighteen months away. The good news was I had plenty of time to save the money as well as plenty of time to lose the pounds

Another opportunity arose to pack the bags in June. Paul's youngest brother, who also has Parkinson's disease and whom I have always loved dearly, lives in California. I hadn't seen him since 2007 when their mother died. I hadn't seen him since his diagnosis, and I really needed to hug him again. Paul's other brother's son was getting married in Spokane, Washington, so I decided to combine those two reasons to travel. It was a whirlwind five days, filled with family and socializing and definitely exhausting and very emotional. Seeing his brother dealing with the same challenging disease as Paul's brought back a multitude of bad memories and emotions. But at least I got to spend quality time with him after such a long time.

The wedding was gorgeous and again emotional. I found I was still not very much in control at weddings, seeing the happy couple so in love and embarking on their new life together, their first chapter. There is no way to not remember those same feelings fifty-two years ago. But the toughest moment came at the reception where there was a poster next to the sign-in book. There was Paul's photo looking at me along with all the other relatives who were no longer with us. It was an unexpected shock to see his face there, and once again I had to leave the room to compose myself. I wondered when these moments were going to stop. How many more times would I embarrass myself with uncontrollable tears? The second anniversary of his death was a few weeks away, and I was very disappointed to still be so out of control after all that time.

My daughter picked me up at the airport the following day, and when I got in her car she said, "Oh, Mom, I am so glad you're home." And I burst into tears again. It was like a floodgate opened up, and all the emotions I had been stuffing down for five days just had to break through the dam. I was never so glad to be home, and on the flight back, I realized something important.

As I looked out the window of the plane at the beautiful clouds below, feeling 36,000 feet closer to Paul, I realized that I was at peace with my life. Yes, I missed him, and yes, I was alone more than not, but I was at peace with it. I thought about how much I loved my fairy tale house and how grateful I was to have it, even though I lived there alone; but I was at peace with it. I realized how lucky I was to have all my family no more than five minutes away, and that I would probably never be lonely because of that blessing. I was at peace with the word "alone".

Then the unexpected happened. The corona virus pandemic hit the United States, and the entire world had to figure out how to cope with this new threat. After a few weeks of somber news reports, the Governor of Ohio issued the order to "stay at home" in order to practice social distance. All non-essential business had to close, and anyone in the senior citizen age group was instructed to be very cautious. This was especially true for those with underlying medical conditions. At least aches and pains weren't an underlying condition! But I still had to give up spending any time with my children and grandchildren. This was particularly difficult since they all lived so close, and I always relished any time I could be with them. My beauty salon closed; my massage therapist canceled my appointments; the physical therapist did the same. No one could go to a movie, a restaurant or a gym. Everything was closed. Symphonies, concerts and ballets were cancelled. All social activities stopped. Anyone with whom I had any regular contact was now off limits. This was really "alone" time. When the Canadian government finally closed their borders, my travel company had no choice but to cancel my much anticipated trip to the Arctic. Suddenly, I found myself reexamining my feelings about being alone. I felt sad, teary all the time especially when I thought about not being with my family. I found myself feeling jealous of anyone who still had a spouse to share a home; I was even jealous of my children for having the luxury of kids with them, noise in their houses, company to share long days and evenings. My little dog was a great companion, but she didn't add much to the conversation! The word "alone" was taking on a whole new feeling, and I didn't like it at all. I felt like a hypocrite who wasn't able to live the lessons I thought I had learned. Suddenly the conclusions I thought I had reached about being at peace with living alone felt like a lie.

Finally after having my personal pity party, I decided that since contact with another human being suddenly felt so important, I would make the effort to email several people every day, and phone someone with whom I had not talked in a while. I took the dog for her daily walk, and it was amazing how many neighbors were out doing the same. Suddenly everybody was walking, jogging, or riding a bike yet keeping social distance. I met neighbors I had never seen before who were also walking their dogs and we kept our social distance. Easter was particularly difficult since for the very first time, there would be no Easter family luncheon or grandchildren egg hunt. The spring house decorations would not be enjoyed by anyone else, and I was terribly sad. Then, like a gift from God, the kids decided to use the Zoom technology on our phones and have a video family chat time on Easter. I sat at my dining room table decorated for Easter and watched the entire family and listened to the familiar family banter, pretending they were all sitting there with me. Then my son suggested we repeat this family time every Sunday while the "stay at home" order was in place. The moments of sadness and tear shedding soon ended, but it had been an interesting time of new reflection on the words "alone" and "lonely".

-Seven-

GUILT!

"Guilt"! Now there's another interesting word worth examining! When I was studying psychology, there was a theory that all stressors in life are caused by only four things: Guilt, Loss, Loneliness and Failure. I had thought about that theory a lot, trying to imagine anything stressful that could be caused by something else other than those four words. I concluded that the theory was in fact correct. Each one of us finds just one of those more stressful than the other three. In my younger years, before I had suffered the loss of anyone I loved, my Achilles heel was failure. I already mentioned that I was rarely, if ever, lonely, guilt hadn't plagued me yet, but failure was something our family never tolerated. We were always expected to succeed at whatever we tried to do, and I always did, until I took my eight hour Master's Degree exam. I failed two out of the eight hours thereby necessitating a re-take three months later. I was so devastated by my failure. I went into hibernation so as not to have to explain to anyone that I had failed. I lost weight and dreaded having to study again to re-take the exam. It was the first time I had experienced failure, and I found out I don't handle it well at all.

Psychologists also point out that some life experiences can be caused by a combination of more than one of these stressors at the same time, like a divorce, which can combine loss with a possible sense of failure and even loneliness. And if guilt set in because of something that caused the divorce, well, that would be the absolute worst case scenario.

I think most women would agree that guilt just comes with motherhood! It's a package deal. It's not fair; it doesn't seem to accompany fatherhood, but for some reason, mothers can always find something to feel guilty about. What's more, it's not a question of genuine, well deserved guilt. All that is needed is the perception that there is a reason to feel guilty whether that is true or not.

My first job out of college was teaching French in a Catholic high school. I had known the nun who hired me since childhood. She became the Principal at the school where I was going to begin my career. The summer before my second year, Paul and I got married. When I began that September, the Principal had changed. Now another nun I had known in high school had the job, and I hadn't been terribly fond of her nor she me. I had been given a one year contract, and at the conclusion of that year it was time to discuss renewal. She had no reason not to renew me, but something she said took me completely by surprise. "I'll renew the contract, but I must say that if I had been the one hiring last year, I wouldn't have hired you!" I was too stunned to say anything, but she continued. "You're getting married over the summer, and now you'll probably get pregnant and have to leave." Of course in today's society, no employer would be able to get away with saying something like that. And what happened? In February, I got pregnant and had to tell her I was leaving! Fortunately, it wasn't just because of the pregnancy. Paul's new job required we move out of town. But I still remember the guilt when I told her, and I hadn't even delivered a baby yet!

Children as they grow up always know how to push our buttons. It doesn't take much to make us question our parental judgment, and anytime there is a perceived flaw in one of our kids, it has to be because of something we did wrong. Why do we do that to ourselves? I grew up in the generation when most mothers didn't work outside the home. I always said I had the best situation ever; my mom didn't work outside the home and my grandmother lived with us. It was like having two stay-at-home mothers, and I must admit I had an idyllic childhood. After saying *au revoir* to the nun and giving up my first teaching job, I loved staying at home with my baby. Paul and I had three kids in five years, and there was no way I was going back to work for a while! In fact it took twelve years before the youngest was in first grade. But when she was three, I had an opportunity to go to graduate school to get credits required to renew my teaching license. Since Paul worked at the university, the tuition was free, and I couldn't pass it up. My mom watched the younger two children when I went part time to classes. Eventually I got the credits to renew my certificate, but I continued on until I could complete my Master's degree. I found my workload overwhelming, keeping a big house, taking care of my kids and studying again after so many years of being away from all that. One day I began to question why I was putting myself through it. When I picked the kids up at my mother's, I began to cry uncontrollably.

"What am I doing? I had a great life because you were always at home with us. I'm killing myself to get these credits so I can get a teaching job that will then take me away from home and my kids!" I was miserable, prematurely guilty of family neglect! I have to laugh when I think of that conversation now, but at the time, it was a very real emotion. On the other hand, maybe I was just exhausted and fed up with studying and trying to talk myself out of finishing. But my mother would have none of it. She said she didn't pay for my college education so that I could stay at home with children. Besides, teaching was the perfect job for a mother with summers off when the kids were home, working while they were in school and home when they are home. That helped, and I knew she was right. As luck would have it, I found the perfect job when all the kids were in school. It was part time, and I was home to put them on the bus and home before they walked in the door. No more guilt...until the first time one of them got sick, and I had to turn the parenting over to my mother. That guilt was something I just had to learn to deal with for many years, and it never got easier.

I retired after twenty-five years of teaching in 2003; Paul had been diagnosed with Parkinson's disease in October, 2000 and that news rocked both our worlds. He continued to work for six more years, we traveled extensively making good use of whatever time he had left to do so; we had eight grandchildren in nine years, and I was helping to babysit for each family one day a week. Then in 2009, Paul opted to have the deep brain stimulation surgery to help control the progression of the disease. The procedure eventually did what it was supposed to do, but not before the surgeon nicked a blood vessel which produced a slow brain bleed causing a ten week rehabilitation. My gut had told me before the surgery to not have it; it was extremely dangerous, and I was terrified, but it was his disease, and he had to make the final judgment. After the outcome was so serious, my guilt kicked in again. "Why did I let him do this? Why didn't I tell him I thought it was too dangerous?" Guilt, guilt, guilt.

Paul retired in March, 2006, and we began planning for his big retirement dream trip, a Mediterranean cruise. My mother had moved in with us in 2002 after my dad died, and she became seriously ill right after Paul retired. Suddenly, our fabulous Mediterranean cruise which was to begin in September was looking doubtful because she became more seriously ill in July and was hospitalized with double pneumonia. We nearly lost her, but somehow this ninety-five year old lady rallied and was released after twenty-one days. She had to go to a nursing home for rehabilitation, and all was going well. I spent hours with her daily; she was amazing everyone on the staff with her recovery...until she became very ill again. Our cruise was only a week away; I wanted to cancel it even though I felt guilty doing that to Paul, but she would not have it.

"I will not allow you to cancel that trip, and there will be no tears when you leave!" The tone of her voice indicated that the conversation was over! So we went, and she died while we were gone. I have never felt such crushing, overwhelming guilt in my life.

After Paul's illness became more advanced nearly ten years

after my mother died, there were so many incidents that caused me enormous guilt that word could have become my middle name. I cared for him the best I could, but no matter what I did, I felt like it wasn't enough; not enough to keep him safe, not enough to keep him comfortable, and he made me so angry at times that I would lash out at him in a rage. Whenever this happened, I would beat myself up with guilt for my lack of compassion. The cycle was most unhealthy for me and certainly not good for him. My daughter sent me an email with a link to some articles written by another woman whose husband had Parkinson's disease. One of them still stands out in my mind. The title was *It's Ok to be Angry*". Really? It was really OK? I reread the article several times, and by the last reading, I could feel the guilt begin to dissolve. Not that my angry responses were justified, but they were normal in my situation. I was human, and when I was tired, I was not always in control.

When he lay dying, drugged with morphine given compassionately by Hospice, I whispered in his ear all the things I was sorry for. Things I had said in anger, things I had done, anything and everything that might have made his last months on the Earth more difficult. A few weeks after his death, my French class with the retirees program was about to begin. It was the first time in years I could go without the stress of wondering if he would be okay while I was gone. My morning was relaxed, I slept a little later, I didn't have a need for my phone to be handy in case I got a call to rush home, and I had a wonderful morning at the university. I was flying high on my drive home, happy to have shared an enjoyable time with likeminded people. And then it happened...The guilt, the overwhelming guilt, because it was at that moment I realized I had enjoyed myself more than I had in years...because he was gone.

When I talked later with my friend, the head nurse with Hospice, who had spent so much time with him the last two years of his life, I confessed to her the guilt I still carried with me. She listened to my confession with love in her eyes, and she told me that Paul and she had talked a week before his death. He told her he knew he was dying but not to tell me. She said that she knew it, too, and she would not betray his wishes. But she also told me that he said he was not afraid to die, that he had had a good, long life. She told me how much he loved me, and she added that I should stop carrying around guilt he would not want me to carry. She told me I had enjoyed myself at the university not because he was gone, but because the stress of caregiving was gone. I was in tears with relief, but it didn't all go away immediately. However I knew there had to be a better path to follow, one that was more positive, one with more self-compassion, something with which I hadn't been very familiar. It was finally time to get acquainted with this emotion.

-Eight-

STARTING ANEW

By the time the second anniversary of Paul's death rolled around, the moments of intolerable grief were becoming farther apart. I still dreamed about him frequently, and these journeys into the unconscious were really a mixed bag of emotions. Sometimes he was young and healthy, walking unassisted, and I would wake up feeling good that maybe he had chosen to visit me that night. In other dreams he was ill and needing assistance for everything, but refusing to use his walker, falling like he had done so many times. I would awake much stressed, and in my sleep filled mind I would think *Go away; I don't want to remember this dream. I don't want to remember you like this.* But I always would remember it in the morning, and it would cloud my day. There were dreams when I could almost feel like I could touch him again or dreams when I could feel his arm around me, but then there were dreams when I would be angry and yelling at him. In one good dream, I could actually see his cagey smile and the twinkle in his eye when he would get caught doing something he knew I didn't like. It was a look I hadn't seen in many years and it flooded my head with memories. I never knew what precipitated any of these dreams. All I knew was that he lived in my sub-conscious and would probably be there forever and having his way with my mind.

At the onset of my third year of widowhood, something changed, and it wasn't good. It was August, hot and humid necessitating any outdoor activities be done in the morning hours. I tried to get out and walk the dog before it got too hot, an activity both of us looked forward to, but for some reason, that bit of exercise didn't lift my spirits. It was also a time of terrible national news with several mass shootings in one week. These have always upset me terribly, starting with Columbine when I was still teaching high school. I used to have nightmares about what I would do to keep my students safe, where I would go, what that stress would be like. And with every shooting since then, the news accounts inevitably moved me to tears.

Just about the same time as the shootings, I began to slip into a serious funk, a mental cloud hanging over me that I couldn't explain. Other than the national news, there was no explanation for why I felt so low. Nothing inspired me to get moving. I didn't feel like seeing anyone nor doing anything, and I have to admit that it frightened me a little. I had thought I was over the hump of serious grief, so why was I feeling so depressed? It also coincided with the early presidential debates, and I was obsessed with learning all I could about each candidate. My favorite was Joe Biden, and I watched an interview with him shortly after the shootings. The question posed was, "In light of all the personal loss you have suffered losing family members, what would you say to the families who lost someone in these shootings?" Joe remained silent for a minute, weighing his words carefully. The he responded slowly. "I would say that there is nothing that can take away your pain. There is nothing anyone can say or do to make it hurt less. Only time can do that, so you just have to lean into the pain. But I would also say that when the time is right, you have to remember what you were passionate about before this loss and try to find it again."

There was the answer to my question. That's what was wrong...I had lost passion for everything, and it was time to try and rediscover it. So, list maker that I was, I tried to remember all the things I had been passionate about before Paul died and even before he got so sick. It wasn't a long list so it shouldn't have been too hard to accomplish this re-discovery. And so, just like my New Year's resolution lists, I began to jot down former passions followed up with strategies to find them again. It was obvious that lifting the funk would require action.

The first item on the list was my passion for the French language and culture and teaching my class at the university. The first week of class was still nearly two months away, but there was always a lot of preparation in planning the eight week syllabus. I could begin immediately and get one complete seventy-five minute class well prepared every week, including the handouts I always provided. This actually took quite a bit of time, and I always enjoyed the preparation process. It was a good way to begin lifting the cloud. And I loved the interaction with these retirees who also loved the language and wanted to improve their skills.

The next item to re-discover was writing my children's books. There were two manuscripts finished and just sitting in my Word documents, waiting for me to try to get them illustrated. I phoned my girlfriend who had just retired from teaching art and set up a date for lunch. When we met, I gave her a copy of the manuscript which was a memoir about the seven trips to France with my students over the course of my career. I asked her to read it and see if she would be interested in doing some sketches to include. She didn't say no, and she was willing to see what inspiration she could find.

The second manuscript was the fourth chapter book in a series for middle school students about French history. It was the true story of Marie Antoinette's four children. I called the man who had illustrated the first three books and asked him if he was up for another. He said yes, but his time was limited. The finished product could be over a year away. I said that was okay. Little by little, I could feel the funk lifting. It was then that I began writing this memoire, examining and reflecting on this new state of life since writing has always been good therapy for me. What else could go on this list?

Travel! Of course, travel had been a passion for both Paul and me for years. Giving it up had been one of the hardest parts of his deterioration. I had already booked my first solo trip for August of 2020 to the Arctic so I really wasn't looking to search for any other destinations, but as luck would have it, the travel company we had always used sent me an email announcing a brand new voyage and brand new ship ready to launch in 2021. It just happened to be one of the unfinished bucket list itineraries that Paul would have loved. But who plans a trip two years away? I nearly deleted the email, but didn't. I read every detail about this beautiful voyage to the British Isles, Ireland, Scotland and Wales for three days in a row. I could not get it out of my mind, and so I called. They were allowing ten of their regular sized cabins to be booked by single travelers, and six of them were already booked! I have never been this impulsive in my life, but I plunked down my deposit and booked the trip for 2021. I was almost giddy with excitement.

The following day, my girlfriend in Colorado called to chat, and I told her about this trip. I casually threw out the question, "Do you want to go?" She said she'd like to see the itinerary. The following day she phoned again and said, "Guess what? I have the stateroom next to yours. I'll meet you in London in 2021!" Now I was really excited, and I realized how very essential it was to have something to look forward to.

With September right around the corner, I knew the Cincinnati Ballet Season was coming up, another of my passions, and Paul and I had gone to every one for decades. I could begin now to offer his ticket to my kids and grandkids. And when school started at the end of August, all their sporting events and concerts would begin to fill up my calendar as they had in years past.

The last item on my list was girlfriend time. So, just as I had done after Paul died, I started lining up luncheon dates for some social connection. Then I made an interesting discovery. It really wasn't anything earth shattering, but it brought home an important point for me. When I had looked at my calendar after Paul's second anniversary at the end of July, there was nothing written on it for the entire month of August. And as a person living alone, the lack of human interaction was obvious. Who knew I needed people so much? It took this introvert by surprise

After making this bit of effort, I could feel myself returning to a more normal mental state. I realized just how easy it could be to slip into a state of depression and how tough it could be to pull out of it. I was grateful that I had heard Joe Biden's interview. But what was this mental state? Was it happiness or something else?

When was the last time you asked yourself if you were happy? What exactly is happiness? I remember a book my mother gave me when I was a sullen teenager. It was called *Happiness Can Be A Habit.* The book suggested that the habit of being happy can be learned. I found this quite helpful when I would slip into a state of teen angst. Webster defines happy as "fortunate, having, showing or causing great pleasure or joy" So was I happy? My family made me happy whenever I was fortunate to be spending time with them, and I knew I was fortunate to have all of them living so close to me. Teaching made me happy whenever I was in a classroom. Writing made me happy, and had done so all my life. So again, I had to ask myself, was I happy? After giving this much thought, I came to the conclusion that there is a subtle difference between happiness and contentment. I don't think any widow can honestly say she is happy with the state of being without her life partner. One cannot be 100% happy with such an upheaval in life. It is never a choice anyone would make, and it is the reason it ranks as number one on the list of stressors in life. But the real question was "Am I content?" Webster's definition says it all, "Satisfied with one's lot." Would I ever choose this lot in life, to go through the next few decades alone? The answer was a resounding NO. But based on his definition, the answer was YES! It is the hand I was dealt, and I could choose to be satisfied with it or to be miserable. I was content, because I was fortunate enough to have figured out a way to make the most of the situation. What more can any of us do?

-Nine-

SETBACKS

It never ceased to amaze me how God continued to take care of me. How sad we don't always recognize His plan until later when we look back on a sequence of events and somehow it all makes sense. Two months into my third year of widowhood, just such a sequence occurred, and the outcome really rocked my world.

It began with moving some heavy furniture, never a good idea in our later years, but the denial of what I thought I could still do was laughing at me again. The day after this event, my back grabbed me as I got out of bed and screamed at me to go to my trusty chiropractor as soon as possible. The adjustment didn't hold, and I had to return the following day. It helped a little, but not much, and the weekend was upon me. For two days, I sat on ice, accomplished absolutely nothing around the house and emptied a wine bottle. Nothing helped.

On Monday, I went for my weekly massage and walked in bent practically in half from the pain. The masseuse took one look and said, "What in the world happened?" I told her and tried to hold back the tears but couldn't accomplish that. Ninety minutes of deep tissue massage later, I got off the table and felt like I could stand up straight, but the pain was still there in my left hip. She told me to drink lots of water to flush out the toxins she probably released into my blood stream. I took her advice, but apparently the wine I added to the mix that night negated the benefits of the water! That night I was in so much pain, sick to my stomach and running a slight fever, all of which I found out later were symptoms of "toxic flu". *Who ever heard of toxic flu?* And back to the chiropractor I went, again in tears. This time she did an ultrasound treatment after the adjustment, but nothing helped. A fourth treatment accomplished nothing again, and I decided it was time to get another opinion at the orthopedic center.

It had been a week since the furniture move, and an X-ray showed nothing alarming at all, but I received an injection of a non-steroidal anti-inflammatory drug to calm things down and also an oral steroid pack to take for six days. The relief was minimal, but it was taking the edge off a bit, and it was also giving me terrible stomach pain. What I didn't need was more pain in the front to keep company with the pain in my back! After six days, I returned for the follow-up appointment. "How are we feeling now, on a scale of one to ten," she cheerfully asked, "compared to how you were when you first came?" Let me just add here that one of my pet peeves is hearing a doctor include herself in the pronoun 'we'. But I answered without dripping too much sarcasm into my response, "We are about a two or a three compared to the twelve we were six days ago. But we are not out of pain!" She decided that there was nothing else she could do without ordering an MRI to get a better idea of what was going on. So two days later, I hobbled into the MRI room, climbed into the tube, closed my eyes so as not to see how claustrophobic it was, tried to count the seconds to see if I could predict when the pounding would stop and wondered why she asked me what kind of music I would like to hear for the next forty-five minutes. What I couldn't figure out was what difference the music could make when the pounding drowned it out completely!

Another weekend came and went with no improvement. I skipped going to church since the thought of sitting for an hour on a hard pew was totally out of the question. I missed the opening night at the ballet and gave my tickets to my daughter so she and her husband could have a date night. And then it was finally time to get the results of the MRI which showed nothing to explain my pain but did re-enforce the fact that my back was getting old! I guess that was a good news/bad news appointment. The serious things they were looking for were not there, and I was glad I hadn't really known what those things were, but I still had no answers. She told me to start physical therapy as soon as possible to strengthen my muscles.

Meanwhile I had my yearly appointment with my GI doctor to check on the colitis issue he had diagnosed two years earlier after Paul died. And herein lies where God was taking care of me. If I hadn't moved the furniture and hurt my back, I wouldn't have needed the steroids. And without the steroids, I wouldn't have had any stomach pain. And without the stomach pain, I wouldn't have had anything to report to the GI doctor. I would simply have said, "All is well; see you next year." But because I did tell him about the stomach pain, he decided to prescribe an endoscopy to double check for stomach ulcers. Maybe I should have guessed what the results would be given the fact that both my parents had had ulcers. But I was shocked to learn that there were four stomach ulcers that hadn't been there two years before! How could that be? I actually thought the first endoscopy two years earlier would have shown the ulcers since I had been so stressed for so long taking care of Paul. But nothing had shown up. Why now, I wondered, two years after his death, would they appear?

So there I was, stomach still not feeling great, incurable colitis that was at least under control, an aging back that hurt even more since I had started the physical therapy the day before, and to make matters worse, because of the ulcers, I had to discontinue the medication for my arthritis that I had been taking for decades. It was overwhelming! My entire body was angry with me.

That evening I sat on my screen porch, lit a candle and had a long talk with myself, with Paul and with God. Again, I asked myself how this could have happened. Why would I have developed four ulcers in the last two years when I thought I had been doing pretty well? It didn't make sense to me at all. All kinds of questions popped into my mind, questions that were not easy to answer, if it was possible to answer them at all. I had always been a strong believer in the mind/body connection, and I wondered if I had been lying to myself in the two years since Paul died about how well I was doing? I realized there is no right way to grieve, and I had chosen a way by plowing through the grieving process in a manner that worked for me, or so I thought. I took the advice that to get through grief, you have to lean into it. I had been leaning hard for two years and thought I had made it to the other side. I had worked so hard to prove I could do this "life alone thing", but did I really believe it? I began to wonder if I had duped myself into thinking I was finally content when my stomach was not buying it. My body obviously wasn't doing as well as I thought my mind was, and that reality scared me to death. I began trying to digest these thoughts and make sense of them, but I was suddenly so confused, I began to cry harder than I had in a long time. I prayed out loud, "Dear God, please help me to get my mind and my body on the same page. I'm not sure any longer that I am capable of living well without Paul." When I said those words out loud, I was suddenly filled with incredible sadness, newfound doubt in my abilities to forge ahead and debilitating fear for what would be in store for me if I couldn't. It was the lowest moment I had felt in a long time, and I didn't know how to get through it. The thought of going to a grief counselor really didn't appeal to me; I felt like I had already gotten through the worst of the process. This felt like a different kind of crisis I had to work through alone. Then I began thinking about the friends I had helped during their personal losses over the past two years, friends who had also read my memoir and told me how much it had helped them during their caregiving journey. I had taken it as a sign that I could make something positive out of my experience for others. But after receiving the news of the ulcers, I began to question why I thought I could help anyone else when I hadn't even been able to keep myself together physically. It became a downward spiral of self-doubt that brought me to tears every time I thought about it.

The following morning, I continued my self-analysis. Okay, I thought, so I have four ulcers, my entire body hurts, and I have to do something to take care of myself. Would I still have gotten the ulcers if I had done anything differently these last two years? If I hadn't pushed so hard to sell the house, find another one and move as quickly as I had, would I have avoided getting ulcers? If I hadn't pushed myself to plan traveling alone and done it even though I didn't entirely enjoy it, would I have still gotten ulcers? Would my body have been any happier if I had just slowed down and not taken on so much? Of course, I would never know the answers to those questions, but the fact was that was just the way I operate. Give me a goal, formulate a plan, make my lists, forge ahead and get it done! Apparently, my brain liked that M.O. but my body didn't. But it was too late to change what was already done. Besides, I loved my new house; it brought me pleasure every day. I was proud of myself for putting fear aside and booking some big international trips even though I'd probably be terrified the nights before departures. And given the fact that I had moved from my parents' home to a home with Paul which we shared for fifty years, and that I had never lived alone before he died, I was also proud of myself for proving I could do it. My stomach may not have liked it, but my brain had said "job well done".

Two days later, I learned another friend who had been the caregiver for her husband for years had become a widow that morning. She had read my book the previous year and wrote me a beautiful letter afterwards thanking me for all the messages she got from it which she would draw on until her difficult job was over. I was so moved, I kept the letter. I went to her house to express my condolences but didn't see her. Rather her son talked with me and said he would tell her I had come by. Later that night, she phoned to thank me for the moral support and for being such a good friend. She recognized that I was probably the only one of her friends who really understood the kind of day she had just lived through. Then she said she would like to sit down soon and have lunch together and talk. The timing was amazing. Just when I had questioned whether I had any business trying to help anyone through their time of emotional loss, God sent me a sign that He still wanted me to continue trying to help.

After finding out about the impossibility of taking my arthritis medication, I went to see my primary care doctor to ask for suggestions on how to remedy this problem. I shared with him my feelings of questioning my success in plowing through the grieving process. I wondered if he thought the ulcer diagnosis was caused by the stress of grief and transitioning into the single life. It was his opinion that it had been a reaction to all the anti-inflammatory medication I had been taking for so long. His assessment was that the family history of ulcers probably increased my sensitivity for them which the latest bout of steroids had made worse. He reassured me that ulcers can heal in six to eight weeks with the proper care and that after that time had passed, we could talk about different approaches to the arthritis problem. I immediately felt better.

I concluded that it didn't really matter why the ulcers had happened; they did, and now I simply had to take care of the situation. I would continue to be present to the friends who sought out my help, but it was also time for a new project, time to make a new list, a list of ways to take care of myself and get healthy again. Suddenly, nothing was more important.

-Ten-
AVAILABLE?

At the funeral visitation for my girlfriend's husband, I was talking to several mutual friends when my nephew walked into the church. He was good friends with the deceased's son. I went up to him to say hello, and he casually asked, "Are you flying solo today?" The question took me by surprise, and I answered, "How else would I be flying these days?" I thought, *of course I'm flying solo; I have been for over two years now.* But the innocent question got me thinking.

Shortly after my former neighbor's wife died, another girlfriend called me on the phone to make a lunch date. A few moments into the conversation she playfully said, "Well, I hear your next door neighbor is available now!" I didn't get it; I thought *my next door neighbor is a guy from Bulgaria; what's he available for?* Clueless, I asked "What are you talking about?" Then she laughed and said, "You know, your former neighbor who just lost his wife." I was so stunned when I realized what she was suggesting; I was speechless for a moment but finally collected myself and probably said something stupid that I don't really even remember. But I wondered if this was going to be the common assumption from people after someone is widowed? And even though I knew she meant no harm, I was momentarily offended. But why, I later asked myself, was I offended? What did her comment imply, and why did it hit me wrong? She had only been kidding around; had I lost my sense of humor as well as my husband? And so began a bit more self-analysis.

Shortly after my former neighbor's wife died, I saw him in the grocery store. We chatted briefly about how he was doing. I asked him what he was doing to help himself through the tough days he was facing. When he said he had been trying to get together with friends for lunch or dinner, I said, "Well don't forget I'm a friend, too." Then I laughed. "I'm not asking you on a date, just coffee and conversation if you ever need it." His response was, "Well, it wouldn't do you any good if you were asking." It was important to me to let him know I wasn't coming on to him.

I thought back to that brief but important exchange when he finally took me up on the invitation and asked if he could come over for coffee some morning. As I wrote earlier, it was very therapeutic for him, and I knew we would meet again. About a month later, we were attending the same Sunday Mass. At the sign of peace when we usually shake hands with the people around us, he left his pew, came up to mine and said, "I need a hug today." I was totally shocked, gave him a hug, and with tears in his eyes, he said he would call me soon.

Our second coffee together was very intense; he had much on his mind and really needed to talk it all out. I said a quick prayer to the Holy Spirit to inspire me to say the right words to help him. In the course of our long conversation, I shared with him the phone conversation with my girlfriend suggesting that he was now available and how that had offended me. Then he brought up our brief conversation in the grocery, but it was what he said about it that surprised me. He admitted he had been very relieved to have the clarification that I just wanted to continue being his friend. But there it was again; in the back of his mind was the possibility that I wanted more from him since we were both recently widowed.

As I began to analyze why all this offended me, I began to examine the implications of those attitudes. For starters, it assumed I was actually looking for someone to take Paul's place in my life, and nothing could have been farther from the truth. In fact, no one could ever take on that role successfully. I had been on my own for two years, and as I wrote earlier, I had learned to become quite content with the hand I had been dealt. Perhaps the people who made comments like the one my friend had made were actually admitting that if they were in my place, they wouldn't be content living alone and just assumed I felt the same way. And as for my former neighbor, even though he wasn't looking for someone to take his wife's place, he may have been afraid that I was looking to take on that role and was relieved to know I wasn't.

I think I had also been offended because there was the assumption that I couldn't make it on my own as a single woman, that I needed a man to help me get through the rest of my life. My mind immediately conjured up the images of the poor widow in Scripture, vulnerable to all the perils of living alone. Excuse me, but I don't think so! Had there been times when I felt anxious about something, a strange noise outside, a power outage leaving me alone in the dark? I admit, shortly after Paul died when I was getting used to being alone in that big house, there had been a few times I had been a little afraid. But I managed to get through them. Since living in my new home, there had been no such incidents; besides I had a fearless protector in my vigilant little watchdog! She didn't miss a thing!

Nor did I need the additional income from a husband to help me survive my station in life. For years before Paul died, especially when I saw the handwriting on the wall, I had begun a fiscal program that served me well. Ever since his botched brain surgery in 2009, I had learned to take on paying all the bills and also managed to get us through some major hurdles during the recession. Though that was a budgeting nightmare at the time, I did it. Granted I needed my banker/son-in-law's help to show me how to get it done, but I did it. I became obsessed with saving, and I made copious lists to plan how to get by after Paul's eventual death. I paid off the credit cards, cancelled them after each was paid off and ceremoniously cut them up, one at a time. After his death, his life insurance, added to the selling price of my home, made it possible for me to buy a new and less expensive house and live comfortably. With both our retirement benefits, I was doing just fine.

The bottom line, I concluded, was that I had learned I really wasn't in the market to share this new phase of my life with anyone. I had learned to enjoy my freedom to do what I wanted, when I wanted without being accountable to anyone else. I couldn't foresee ever living with another man whose health could possibly take a bad turn, making me a caregiver again and then leave me vulnerable to grieve a second time. That kind of profound loss should never be experienced more than once! If that was a foreign concept for my friends who still had a spouse, well, so be it. If God had different plans for me, I would just wait for them to become crystal clear. The suggestion that someone was "available" for me to pursue would possibly come up again, but if it did, I wouldn't be offended. But I would be better prepared to nip the conversation in the bud! Instead of being offended, I should probably thank my girlfriend for the motivation to examine my position on this subject.

-Eleven-

CEMETERIES

hy is it that some people have no problem going to cemeteries and others, like me, have an aversion to them? When my maternal grandmother, who lived with us and was like a second mother to me, died in 1966, I was distraught beyond words. My sister and brother-in-law were living in Germany with the Army, and I felt an enormous responsibility to help my mother through her grief. Years before her death, when I was much younger, my parents bought three cemetery plots, one for my grandmother and one for each of them. Any time my mother decided it was time to put flowers on the graves of other relatives I would have to go with her. I never understood why it was necessary to do that. Who were the flowers really for? Certainly not for the loved ones buried six feet under! Inevitably, we would have to walk past the three purchased plots, headstones included with names and birthdates already there, and it would send me into a profound sadness. It was as though those three pieces of marble were just waiting to add the death dates of all the people I loved. It felt so macabre to me, and I could hardly look at them. Then in 1966, one of them finally got to add the date of my grandmother's death. I remember looking at the headstone and thinking *well are you happy now?*

I wasn't touched by the disabling emotions brought on by death again until 2001 when my father died suddenly. Granted he was ninety-five and had lived a long and wonderful life, but his departure turned my world upside down. I cried into my pillow that awful night, thinking about my small family, mom, dad, one sister and me and realized we would never be a complete family ever again. It felt like a limb had been chopped right off my body. His funeral was disconsolately difficult for all of us, and for some reason my mind kept going back to my earliest memory of him. I couldn't have been more than three years old at the beach in Florida. My inflatable fish got swept up in a wave and began drifting out farther and farther into the ocean. I remember crying until my hero waded out, retrieved my fish and saved the day for me. *What a stupid thing to remember,* I thought, as I touched his casket before leaving the cemetery and my hero behind. Now two of those stones had claimed their everlasting, bookend dates.

Of course my mother, being a cemetery visiting person, needed to go frequently to put fresh flowers on his grave and on her mother's, and it was up to me to drive her there. I dreaded the trip every time, especially that first year since she was inconsolable, and I would inevitably be a heap of tears with her. Once again, I had to question why it was so important to her to keep flowers in a little bronze vase next to a piece of marble. She always claimed it was to pay respect to the dead. I still didn't get it, but I continued to take her when she wanted to go, and my hatred of cemeteries grew even more.

Five years later, the third stone claimed its date when my mother died while Paul and I were on his retirement cruise. I thought my world had come to an end. She and I had always been incredibly close, even more so when she lived with Paul and me after my father died. The last four years of her life were in my care, and I couldn't imagine life without her. Every detail of her funeral day is still clear in my head, and none so clearly as the time spent at the cemetery. I felt like my heart was going to stop, it was beating so hard and so fast; I found it hard to breathe as the moment approached to say the final goodbye. I remember putting my hand on her casket, crying at the inconceivable realization that I would never see my mother again. I just couldn't bring myself to leave her there.

Once during one of our many treks to put flowers on the graves, she had indicated that she fully anticipated my carrying on the tradition. It was never a question of if I would put flowers on their graves, but rather an expectation that I would. I never had the courage to tell her that this tradition was probably not going to be passed on to me. Nor would I ever expect my children to do this for me. Perhaps you should go back right now and read the chapter on guilt once more! After her death, I was consumed with it. Was I really disrespecting her by not putting flowers there? I thought back to that last moment when I touched her casket for the last time before leaving the cemetery. I had reluctantly said my goodbyes, and I had no desire to revisit that moment.

My sister, also a cemetery visiting person and a Master Gardener, thankfully took on the role. Not only did she landscape the areas around all three plots with perennial flowers, and beautifully I might add, but she also said she thought it would be a great idea if the two of us combined resources and purchased a concrete bench to put alongside the trio of our dead loved ones. As this was not exactly inexpensive, I had to ask her, "Why would we want to do this?" She had every intention, she said, of visiting during lunch time so she could bring a meal and sit there with them. I told her I would be happy to contribute, but there would never be a way I would find it comforting to eat a sandwich alongside three gravestones wearing the names of the three people I missed more than anyone in the world. I wondered if there was something wrong with me. Her husband said by avoiding the cemetery I was putting off closure. I assured him I had had my closure the day of the funeral. My sister continued the seasonal visits, weeded her perennial garden and put flowers in the little bronze vases. Inevitably, she would text me photos of how the plots looked after her handiwork.

In the eleven years between my mother's death and my husband's in 2017, I never went back to the cemetery unless another relative died, and I was forced to go. I always did my familial duty, but I never did revisit the graves of my parents or grandmother, nor did I ever sit on the bench I had helped purchase. As long as my sister made the four visits each year, weeding the garden and changing the seasonal flowers, I felt less and less guilt for avoiding the scene.

My husband's death in 2017 followed many years of illness and twenty-four-seven caregiving on my part. And just like the details of my parents' and grandmother's funerals, every moment is seared into my heart and soul. He and I had long before decided on cremation, and the sealed, wooden chest containing his ashes rested on a small table in the center aisle of the church, taking up a fraction of the space required for a large, obscenely expensive coffin. This was another hang up I had about death; I found it offensive that a business would profit so handsomely from the grief of loved ones. It just felt so wrong. The day we had to accompany my mother to pick out my dad's casket, I was incredibly angry as I walked around the display room. The prices were outrageous; would my dad even care what kind of box they put him in? None of this felt necessary to me. I remember thinking if I didn't get out of there soon, I might make a scene!

The funeral director asked me at church if I wanted to carry Paul's ashes inside and place them on the little table, a question I wasn't anticipating. This should have felt like an honor but I shuddered at the thought for some reason and politely declined. After the service concluded, I watched the funeral director wheel that mini casket out to the hearse after Mass, and I remember thinking how stupid to use such a large vehicle for such a small wooden box. Even now, in retrospect, it's hard to describe how those feelings affected my perception of what is so readily accepted in our culture. Nothing about all those traditions felt right to me

Our son was my chauffeur that day, and we were in the first car following the hearse. That was the longest, most difficult drive of my life since my church was on the other side of town from the cemetery. For the entire length of the journey I kept thinking about where we were going and dreading the thought of yet another final goodbye at a place I hated. Our plot was not too far from the graves of the other members of my immediate family, and of course, we had to walk past them to arrive at Paul's final resting place. The headstone wasn't there yet; I had taken care of designing it, but it would be weeks before it was finished. The wooden chest was already there awaiting the circle of mourners. All eight of my grandchildren and their parents were there, and I really tried not to cry in front of them. They were already upset enough at losing their dad and their Papa; I didn't want to make them feel worse. I held it together until that final moment that I always dreaded, the moment when it's time to walk away, the time to say the final goodbye. But just like the other times, when I put my hand on the little chest I had to give in to my emotions.

Weeks later the funeral director called to tell me the headstone was in place if I wanted to see it. Oh how I didn't want to go back there! I wanted to say, "I know what it's supposed to look like; I take your word it's done right." But of course, I had to face the moment in a more mature and responsible way. My daughter offered to go with me, and as much as I knew she hated cemeteries, too, I felt I really needed the moral support. As I wrote in the epilogue to the memoire, *In Sickness and in Health,* "we parked the car and walked past the graves of my parents and grandmother and down the slope to where our plot was. I thought I knew what I was going to see, but when I saw his name in big letters with his birth and death dates and my name right under it, I wasn't ready for it, not even a little bit. All I could say was "UGH", like I had been punched in the stomach and had the wind knocked out of me for a moment. I don't know how I thought I was going to feel, but the reality of that moment, the finality of his life after a fifty year marriage, engraved into a stone for all eternity made my knees weak. I dropped to the ground; I tried to talk to him; I needed to tell him how much I missed him, but I also had to tell him I knew I would not come back, could not come back; I saw no reason to spend time with his ashes. That wasn't him. I told him I was sorry, that I didn't mean to disrespect him, but I just couldn't ever return. Then as we walked back to the car, we passed by the concrete bench, and I sat down on it for the first time and gave into the overwhelming emotion. I didn't just cry; I wailed. It seemed to come from a place inside me I didn't even know existed, and I was helpless to contain it. All I remember saying when I could finally catch my breath was, "Why would anyone want to get married a second time and have to possibly experience a loss so profound again?"

My sister continues to visit the graves of our parents, our grandmother and now my husband. She faithfully adorns their plots with flowers of the season and sends me pictures of the results. I still get a knot in my stomach when I see Paul's headstone; I wonder if I'll ever get used to it. But I am grateful to her for doing this since I cannot, nor will I ever have a desire to do it. But what is more important is that I have put all guilt aside. Honestly, I know Paul understands.

-Twelve-

HUMILITY

Two years and four months after losing Paul, and seven weeks after hurting my back moving furniture, I was a month into physical therapy. It was discouraging on so many levels since there were a few good days here and there but more bad days than I was expecting. After four sessions with the therapist and four weeks of doing their exercises at home, I felt the improvement was minimal. Adding to the complexity of the pain problem was the arthritic discomfort resulting from having to stop taking the prescription for that condition thanks to the stomach ulcers. The therapist listened as I described my discouragement and told me that it takes at least four weeks for the new neural connections to be made and only after that will the muscle strength begin to improve. Each time I went to my appointment, I would see small changes for the better, but additional problems would become evident. It was like peeling back the layers of an onion; one layer would reveal something I needed to work on, but then the next would indicate a new area of weakness.

The fourth session was with a different therapist who was covering for my regular therapist who was on vacation. This therapist had also been a ballet dancer as I had been in my youth, and was well aware of many of the physical issues current and former dancers encounter along the way. I told her about a problem I had at the last session completing an exercise, an exercise that should have been easy but which slammed me with way too much pain to be good for me. She understood completely what the problem had been and said we were going to start working on that problem immediately. All the years of my ballet training, turning my feet out from the hip, had allowed my hip flexors to forget how to turn inward without pain. When my toes pointed straight ahead, to me it felt like I was pigeon toed. There was the newest layer of onion peel to tackle. We worked for about half an hour on this one thing alone; it really felt like baby steps which discouraged me even more. As the session wrapped up, she gave me my homework to tackle for the upcoming week. She could tell I was feeling discouraged, and then I made the mistake of sharing with her part of the reason for it. I told her I was afraid that at my age, it would be impossible to get my body to the point where I could be functional and pain free ever again. I told her that I had neglected my own physical health and exercise program for so many years taking care of Paul before he died two years earlier, and the saying "use it or lose it" certainly applied. I had not used the right muscles for so many years, had allowed them to weaken, and I felt I was in pretty sorry condition. But what shook me even more was that I didn't get through this explanation before I began to tear up, leaving me completely out of control emotionally. I was terribly embarrassed, standing in the middle of a therapy room with so many other people working out, but I couldn't stop the waterworks once it started. She was most encouraging and consoling and told me that I could get myself to a point of proper muscle function, even at my age; it just might be at a slower pace than it would be for someone younger. She said even though my years of formal dance training had ended fifty years ago, it still benefitted me today because I had much better body awareness than most of the clients they see, and that made it easier for her to teach me what to do. I thanked her and tried to feel better, but the tears followed me out to the parking lot where I sat for a few minutes trying to collect myself. The inevitable self-analysis followed on the drive home.

That was not the first time I had lost control emotionally after mentioning the many years of caregiving which had prohibited me from taking care of myself. Why was that still such an emotional trigger after nearly two and a half years? I had known there would be moments of renewed grief that would grab me unexpectedly, but this felt like something different. But what was it?

It finally dawned on me after much reflection and soul searching that I was grieving the loss of not just my husband, my life partner, but also the loss of my youth, my stamina, my strength, and my ability to do even the easiest ballet step without pain, whether from muscle weakness or from arthritis. I felt like I had lost not just my soul mate but also a very important part of my own soul, a facet of my life which for years had helped define who I was. It was an unexpected moment of truth that I really didn't like at all, and it hurt, both physically and figuratively. And to add insult to injury, recent scientific research indicates that those who are widowed, male or female, run a higher risk of developing dementia due to the stress of losing a life partner! Well, isn't that great news?

So what was the solution? There was no turning back from the physical therapy even though the original reason for starting had been remedied. The only way to feel better both physically and emotionally was to lean into the pain, just as I had to do after Paul died. But instead of emotional pain, it was physical pain I had to work on, and there was no way to deny it. It wasn't going to be pretty, but if I ever wanted to feel good about myself again, I had to put in the work and get it done! I found myself thinking about a slogan I had heard in the poetry writing workshop I was attending, and it seemed to fit. "Life is like literature; it's never too late to revise!"

About five weeks into the physical therapy, I was beginning to feel better. The therapist had to assess my progress for insurance purposes and discovered that I really was making progress in both flexibility and strength. Suddenly, it didn't seem like I was a hopeless case of old age any longer. But at just about the same time, I did something even more stupid than moving furniture and hurting my back. I fell. In retrospect I know the results could have been much worse than they were, but at the time, I was in a serious amount of pain. I was at the gas station getting ready to refuel before going to my grandson's basketball game. It was raining, and I was running a bit late. I put the nozzle into the car and realized I hadn't selected the grade of gas yet. Rather than remove the hose, or better yet, walk around the front of the car in the rain, I decided to step over the hose. I guess it was higher than I thought because one foot went over it just fine, but the other one didn't quite make it. My body went flying forward, and I ended up face down on the concrete landing hard on my right hip bone and ribs. My arthritic hands and wrists were scraped, and there was blood running down my right shin. My knees were throbbing and my ribs really hurt. What was even more incredulous to me than falling was that every gas pump was occupied, but not one person came to see if I was alright or even to ask me if I was okay. After slowly pulling myself up, I selected the gas and begin filling the tank. It was lucky that I hadn't broken my hip, but I wasn't too sure about my ribs.

When I got to the game, I went into the bathroom and washed the blood off my leg, my knees were already black and blue, as well as a large bruise forming under my right forearm. Though it hurt to breathe deeply, I collected my wits and met my family in the gymnasium. Fortunately, the game only took an hour, and I drove home and put an ice bag on my ribs. Of course, it was a weekend, so I really couldn't do anything about my ribs until Monday unless I went to the ER, and I really didn't want to do that. I had to sleep sitting up because I quickly discovered that if I lay down, I couldn't get up without terrible stabbing pain.

By Monday I knew I had to do something because the pain was excruciating. I decided to go to the after-hours clinic at the orthopedic center for an x-ray which Medicare would pay for. When I signed in, the receptionist asked why I was there, and when I told her, what she said shocked me.

"We don't do ribs after hours."

"What?" I replied incredulously. "Why not?"

Apparently, after hours, the person in charge is a physician assistant, not a medical doctor. If the ribs were broken, there was a risk of puncturing a lung, and they would not be equipped to handle that. If the ribs were just bruised or cracked, there wouldn't be anything they could do anyway. She suggested I go to the emergency room. I couldn't believe it. I translated this to mean that there would be no reason to make a follow-up appointment and charge more money. But maybe that was just being mean spirited! I went to my chiropractor instead and paid for the x-ray which didn't indicate anything obviously broken. But she said even bruised ribs can take four to six weeks to heal!

The following day was my scheduled physical therapy appointment, but there was no way I could do it. She sent me home and said to give it more time to feel better. I told her I didn't know how long that might be, and we might have to suspend the therapy for a while. It was a very low moment for me; *two steps forward, three steps back*, I thought.

When I went for the next therapy appointment, I was still in a good deal of pain. The therapist indicated that if nothing was broken, I shouldn't still be in so much discomfort. She suggested I get a second opinion, and so I went to my family doctor and asked for another set of x-rays. It was eighteen days after I had fallen, and I still believed I hadn't broken anything. The following day the results proved totally different. I had, indeed, three broken ribs! I was shocked, to say the least, but it certainly explained why I had been in so much pain. When I looked back on all the chores I had continued to do despite the discomfort, I had to laugh. It was only weeks until Christmas, and the house had to get decorated. The only help I had was when my grandchildren came over and got the boxes of decorations off the high garage shelf since I couldn't lift them down. I concluded that when you are alone, you just get about doing what you have to do and think about it later!

Over two thousand years ago Cicero wrote, "It is not by muscle, speed, or physical dexterity that great things are achieved, but by reflection, force of character, and judgment." Well, I guess I could take that as some consolation at this point in my life. Many people struggle when they first retire because they feel as if they have lost their identity; as if what they did said who they were. I was never in that category, thankfully. I felt I still had a full and interesting life of caring for grandchildren, travel and volunteering at the local university teaching French to retirees. I was still physically active when I retired in 2003. And it was during retirement that I had begun writing my children's books. But sixteen years later, after these mishaps, I was having a tough time accepting my physical limitations. I certainly had more time for reflection, and muscle speed and dexterity were definitely challenged. But maybe that wasn't so terrible. Muscles and bones would heal, and when they healed I would use better judgment and reflect a bit more before doing something unsafe. And if there is a supplement to take to stave off memory issues, I'll take it! But I thought that if life was indeed like literature, this revision was going to take quite a while!

-Thirteen-

PARTY OF ONE

Culinary talent has never been my strong suit. It's not that I don't like to cook; I've just never been ambitious enough to go out on a limb and try complicated recipes. Add that to the fact that I have been accused all my life of being a very picky eater, not untrue, you can see why the kitchen has never been my favorite room in the house. I was a skinny little kid, and although my mother was a wonderful person, I have to say that I rarely enjoyed her cooking. When I think back to our family dinners, I find myself remembering more entrees that I really detested than those I loved. I mean, what kid likes to eat liver and onions? But I didn't starve so there had to be many that I did like.

When Paul and I got married, the first meal I cooked after our honeymoon was a broiled steak, and I burned it. He was very sweet and did his best to eat every bite. There was really only one other meal I knew how to cook, and that was our family recipe for Rice Krispie Chicken, something hard to mess up. We also had very little money to splurge at the grocery store, so meals in those early days were ridiculously simple. Someone gave me Julia Child's cookbook, *Mastering the Art of French Cooking*, for a wedding present, and now fifty plus years later, it is practically like new.

I got pregnant in the first year of our marriage, and morning sickness became all day sickness for the first three months. I don't remember anything during that time about cooking or even eating except to ingest an entire box of Girl Scout cookie Trefoils on the way home from my first teaching job to keep from throwing up in the car and drinking copious amounts of juice that summer. After becoming a mother and moving out of town for Paul's first job, I tried to branch out in the kitchen. But on May 7th, 1969, a tornado blew part of a roof into the kitchen window, destroying what was on the top of the stove. We were lucky that the three of us were not in the two rooms that blew in, but we had to vacate our home that night, and the National Guard was called in to secure the area. Fortunately, I was nursing my baby and had no need for a stove to warm up formula, and we stayed with friends until we could find another place to live. Those were crazy times to be sure, and I have absolutely no memory of anything I cooked for months following our upheaval.

Four months later, we moved again to Columbus when Paul began his studies for his Ph.D. at The Ohio State University. All he had in the way of money was a student stipend, and I wasn't working outside the home. If I spent more than $20.00 at the grocery each week we had to cut expenses somewhere else. Those were certainly lean times, but in retrospect, they were also good times. Seven years later, we had two more children and an opportunity to move back to Cincinnati for Paul's job as a Ph.D. Immunologist at the University Hospital.

Cooking for a family of five became routine after a while, but again my meals were inexpensive and simple since I was still not working outside the home to add to the budget. I have to chuckle now when I hear my adult children talk about the meals I fixed that they hated. But in my defense, they also recollect that even after I began working outside the home, I still prepared a hot meal for the five of us, and we always ate together, no matter how busy the schedules became. I still take pride in that since today many families don't seem to have that luxury.

After we became empty nesters, I found it challenging for a

while to cook for just the two of us again. But it certainly did help the grocery budget. There were quite a few of my meals that Paul really liked, and I experimented with new things, like cooking in the Crock Pot and preparing meals in the Wok. During the school year when I was exhausted after a day of teaching, the dinner prep went pretty much back to tried and true easy meals, but in the summer, I could give the kitchen more creative energy. And then my mother moved in with us!

We devised a schedule where she would cook three nights a week, I would cook three nights a week, and we would eat out the seventh night. We had very different tastes, likes and dislikes, but dividing the cooking gave both of us a chance to cook what we liked. I admit I had flashbacks to the dreaded meals of liver and onions! She found it extremely difficult to cook on the nights when Paul would have to work late, which was frequently, since we never knew what time he'd walk in. I was used to this, but she would get angry if she thought her meal was ruined when he finally showed up. Many times she'd say in a huff, "I don't know how you put up with this!" Little did she know that before she moved in with us, I'd just make him a sandwich when he got home, and he was fine with whatever I put in front of him. As long as there was a couple of cookies or ice cream for dessert, he was a happy guy. She was appalled when I shared that fact with her, and she intimated that I was neglecting my hard working husband. I knew it was just a generational thing, but that wasn't a pleasant night!

After her death in 2006, Paul was six years into his diagnosis of Parkinson's disease. He also retired that same year, and our meals returned to a more predictable pattern. However, a few years later, after his deep brain stimulation surgery in 2009, he began experiencing the problem of food getting lodged in his esophagus, necessitating trips to the emergency room for an endoscopy. I lost count of the number of times we had to do that, and it was always upsetting. Cooking wasn't enjoyable for me at all, and I struggled to even think of ways to prepare his meals to keep that from happening. Nor could I relax eating a meal with him, because I was always afraid

I would hear him make the dreaded noise indicating that food was stuck. It wasn't choking, something I feared terribly, but rather a sound that indicated he couldn't swallow, not even his own saliva. Toward the last years of his life, I became a master of feeding him food that was easier for him to swallow; he never complained and always ate everything on his plate. In fact, I think the three meals and two snacks he ate every day were the high points of his entire day. Meanwhile, I couldn't seem to keep food in and managed to lose thirty pounds in the last year of his life. We joke now that he would always try to con his caregivers and even our daughter when she would come to relieve me. At 9:00 in the morning he would say to them, "You know this is the time of the day when your mother/ Dee gives me two cookies!" They would always laugh and say they didn't believe that was true.

And then he was gone. No more cooking for five; no more cooking for two. It was just me at the table. This was a consequence of widowhood I had never even considered. Cooking for one? How do you do that? The first time I went to the grocery store after Paul died, I didn't have a clue how to shop for "just me". I remember roaming up and down the aisles not knowing what to put in the cart. It was very unsettling. There were many nights I didn't even feel like eating much less cooking, and it took me a while to realize that I really didn't have to cook if I didn't want to. I didn't even have to eat if I didn't want to. It was actually a bit liberating. If I wanted breakfast for dinner, I could have it. If I wanted wine and munchies for dinner, I could do that. It was months before I figured out a way to shop and prepare a meal for one. Sometimes I would buy a big Ribeye steak, cut it in half and make two meals out of it. I found many frozen dinners for one that were pretty tasty, inexpensive and easy. The freezer section of the grocery became one of my favorite aisles; it was a challenge to find new things to try that were healthy and simple. I was nearly gleeful when I found a package of four small Filet Mignons. It was more expensive, but it gave me one delicious meal over four weeks.

When I visited my girlfriend after her husband died, one of

the first things she said to me was, "I still haven't figured out this cooking for one thing." When I think back to all the helpful advice I read after Paul died, all the suggestions for getting through the many painful firsts, there was never any advice on adjusting to the phenomenon of cooking for one. Maybe I should think about looking for a cookbook that caters to the single person because there is obviously a market for it.

-Fourteen-
OLD-OLD

There was a Swiss philosopher named Henri Amiel who wrote, "To know how to grow old is the master work of wisdom and one of the most difficult chapters in the great art of living." When I read those words I felt that if you substituted the words "to grow old" with the words "to become widowed", the same could be said. Since the majority of widowed people are usually in their golden years, much of his philosophy can be applied to this new state of life that none of us has chosen. And since we didn't choose it, what is important is how we choose to deal with it. It's not an easy transition to make in the art of living. When my former neighbor's wife died, he said to me with passion, "I hate my new station in life!" I understood how he was feeling, and I was hoping he would realize in time that his new station of life had to be accepted, even embraced, to be able to continue on with a meaningful life. I wanted him to eventually come to the conclusion that being widowed is not a disease. It is a time for survival and growth into a new kind of strength. But it takes time.

Gerontologists who study the science of aging divide old age into three categories: the youngest are between the ages of sixty-five and seventy-four. The old-old are between seventy-five and eighty-four, and the oldest old are eighty-five and beyond. My friends and I and all those I know who have recently lost a spouse are in the old-old category. Being in this category need not be a burden although it can feel like one after losing your life partner. Only time can lift that burden, but what is essential, I believe, is that the sooner it is lifted the better. Being widowed and old-old isn't the end; it is simply a new stage in the art of living.

I've given this a lot of thought since I lost Paul. When you really think back to your youth, you have to accept the fact that every phase of life was a new beginning. The terrible two's seemed to repeat themselves in the teen years, to which every parent can attest. Both were just different stages of searching for independence. Every stage after, be it young adulthood or middle age or retirement had its own set of new challenges, new beginnings and new purposes. Getting through school, making and keeping friends or choosing not to keep them, finding a job, excelling at it, making a living that prepared for the future, retiring from the job, all were new beginnings that propelled us into becoming old. Each stage of my life, I believe, has had its own purpose; as a student, it was to learn, to prepare myself academically for the next stage. As a young adult, it was to find my place in society; for me that was in a classroom teaching foreign language. As a parent, it was to rear my children to be productive, independent people, probably the most important job of all. As a teacher, it was to open a new world to teens through a new language. As a grandparent, it was to help and support my children in their role as parents. As a wife and caregiver, it was to support my husband during his career and help him through his illnesses. But now what, now that I have reached the old-old stage and now that I am widowed, what is my purpose now?

I wrote earlier that after Paul died and my days of being a caregiver were over, I had to dig deep to rediscover my new purpose and it was really difficult. But I have come to believe that God expects us to find that purpose in every phase of our lives, whether we are still married or not. There has to be a new purpose because we are still here. Joubert, a French writer and philosopher, said, "The evening of a well-spent life brings its lamps with it." Well, if that's true, then this new station of my life has to be one of enlightenment, and I just have to figure out how to turn on the bulb.

I believe that God has a plan for each of our lives; I admit that takes a strong faith at times since His will is not always in sync with mine. I also do not believe in co-incidence. I believe there is a reason for everything that happens. So if I have been given the gift of a long life, and I guess you can say being in the old-old category is a long life, it must be a part of God's will for me. And if I have to live out my life as a widow, that, too, is part of His plan. But let's face it; we can prepare for old age by being prudent with our finances, making intelligent decisions along the way and taking care of our bodies and our minds, but there aren't lesson plans for preparing for widowhood. It's a transformation in our life that takes some time to get accustomed to. We have the choice to accept or not accept our new role for what it is and come to terms with it. We have to learn how to no longer be half of a couple. That one fact is a work in progress for me since there are still many things I have not done as a widow that I would have done as part of a couple. For example, I used to love going to eat out in restaurants, that is, before Paul's swallowing problems made that stressful. But I can't seem to get myself to go to a restaurant and sit there alone. I used to love to go to movies and theater productions, I still hadn't bought a ticket for one, until recently, and it wasn't a good experience.

Paul and I had gone for years to the traveling companies that brought Broadway productions to Cincinnati. Our favorite was Les Miserables. It was especially important to me since it dealt with French history and whose story was written by my literary hero, Victor Hugo. Paul loved it, too, and we both got completely sucked into the emotion of the story and the incredible genius of the music. We saw it twice in Cincinnati and made sure to it in London when we traveled there. We laughed at the same moments, and we cried at the same moving scenes, made more poignant by the beauty of the music and the amazing talents of those who sang the songs. We used to hold hands during those intense moments, understanding exactly how the other felt.

When Les Mis came back to Cincinnati, I thought about buying one ticket because I couldn't imagine not going, but put it off due to the fact that it would be another "first". Finally, the desire to see it again outweighed the fear of going alone, and I bought a single ticket. The house was a sellout, and I found my seat in the nose bleed section of the theater. By the time the lights went down, every seat in this enormous theater was filled, every seat except one right next to me! I couldn't believe it. It was almost as though it had been reserved for Paul, and I couldn't help but remember the empty seat in Phantom of the Opera reserved for the Phantom himself. Every predictable time I was moved to tears, I wanted to reach over and hold his hand, the phantom hand that wasn't there. By the time the final death scene played out, I had run out of tissues as well as sleeves to wipe my tears. Were they tears of overwhelming love of this story, or tears of overwhelming grief? I know they were tears of both, and I think I missed my husband more at that moment than I had in a long time. I couldn't wait to get out of the theater, into my car and give in to the emotion. I admit, I cried all the way home. I decided later that if I ever went alone to any play, it would have to be one he and I had not seen together.

And travel? Well, I'm slowing trying to get back to that. I can only hope that experience will not repeat the emotion felt in the theater. For me, this has been a time to become more introspective and a time to find strength more in the spirit than in the body.

When I was a teacher, I began each day with this philosophy. I come into contact with around one hundred and twenty students a day. There are one hundred and eighty-four school days in a typical academic year. If I can try to be a positive influence in the life of just one student each day, I should be able to affect the lives of all of them in some way by the end of the year. That shouldn't have been difficult, and I really tried to live by that philosophy every day of my career. I remember the first day of my retirement saying to myself, "What is my new philosophy going to be now for this time in my life?" I came up with the following idea: Every day I will do something good for my body, something good for my mind, something good for my soul and something good for someone else. I examine that list at the end of the day, and most days I feel good about it. Not always, but most of the time. During my caregiving years, it was more difficult. Usually my body and my mind felt the neglect. But I prayed a lot and took good care of Paul, and that was the best I could do.

Since his death, I have seen four other friends deal with the loss of their soul mates. One thing we all have had in common is that their departures have taken a part of us with them. I remember when my father died; my mother said often that she felt like half a person. They had been married sixty-eight years, and my heart broke for her. She not only felt like half a person, she acted like half a person. She found no joy in anything that she tried to fill her time. Even her love of her parish church brought her sadness since she wasn't sitting with my dad in the pew. There was a small spark of happiness when she spent time with her grandchildren and great-grandchildren, but the light in her eyes never fully came back on. After having witnessed this profound sadness for the last five years of her life, I think I had made the decision, maybe unconsciously, that when Paul inevitably left me, I would try very hard not to allow grief to consume me in the same way. It terrified me to think of the consequences. My mother was ninety when my dad died; when Paul died I was only seventy-three, and if I lived as long as my parents, making it to the oldest-old category, that would leave a lot of years to be alone. One of the most important things I did for myself was to return to my retirement philosophy. Do something daily for my mind, my body, my soul and something for someone else. After the dust had settled and life became a bit more normal, I found there really was no excuse for not accomplishing all four goals each day.

But how would I manage to do those four simple things every day? They didn't have to be monumental tasks, just simple things. It shouldn't ever be hard to do something for the soul, like a prayer, making a visit to the chapel for a quick rosary, or reading something of a spiritual nature. Taking part in the Osher Lifelong Learning Institute at the university helped me to do something for my mind, preparing to teach my French classes, reading a book a week, even doing the crossword puzzles in the newspaper every morning satisfied that one. Doing something for my body was as simple as walking the dog every day, taking an exercise class at the YMCA, watching my diet, (I'm still working on that one!) Doing something for someone else was the tricky one to accomplish every day. Family and friendships take time and effort, but I found that after becoming a widow, both became a lifeline for survival. My adult children no longer had the same needs for help that they had when their kids were little, but they still needed advice from time to time when problems arose with one child or another. Sometimes just being available to listen was all that was needed in order to do something for someone else. Picking up the phone and checking in on a friend was an easy thing to do; inviting someone for coffee, taking Christmas cookies to a neighbor, all were easy ways to meet this goal. But all these things required the energy and desire to get outside of oneself and open the window to contact with another person. It sounds easy enough, don't you think? But it wasn't always. And it still isn't. I found in the beginning of this new stage of my life that the burden of being alone was sometimes preferable to using the energy needed to be with someone else. Maybe that goes along with the whole Introvert personality thing, I don't know. We cannot completely change who we are, and I know I have never needed a lot of people around me. But being an introvert, I knew it could be easy to live inside myself. It could be easy to live with past memories and neglect to make new ones, but that is exactly what my mother did, and I refused to repeat that. After things settled down during that first difficult year, I discovered I really did need people after all, be they family or friends. I was actually surprised when I admitted that to myself! It certainly didn't mean I had to fall in love again, but rather falling in love again with life and the opportunities it just might offer if I was willing to be open to them.

I have always loved reading mysteries, and Agatha Christie was the ultimate mystery writer in her day. I read a quote of hers that said, "I have enjoyed greatly the second blooming that comes when you finish the life of the emotions and of personal relationships and find suddenly that a whole new life has opened before you, filled with things you can think about, study, or read about...It is as if a fresh sap of ideas and thoughts was rising in you." She was, at the time, writing about her golden years, not necessarily about being widowed. But everything in that quotation can be applied to this state of life as well. Is it possible to find a second blooming when you finish the life of a fifty year relationship with another human being, when you are plunged suddenly into a new kind of life of solitude? Of course it is possible, but not without making the conscious decision to try.

I want to make a distinction between solitude and isolation. Solitude can be a good thing. It can bring with it time for reflection, a time to think back over our lives, remembering the good and the bad. What are the lessons to take from the past stages of life? What have people in my past taught me about how to navigate this new road ahead? Widowhood has certainly provided more solitude time, more time to find the answers to those questions.

My professors introduced me to a language and culture that continue to this day to bring me enormous pleasure which I love sharing with others. My mother taught me many great lessons over the course of her life; probably the most important one was to never grow old regretting the new things you didn't try because you were afraid. But the last one she taught was how **not** to grieve. I keep that lesson with me now. My dad taught me the importance of hard work and honesty, generosity and by frequently using his favorite quote, "Your attitude is your altitude." What is my attitude about living alone now and how will it shape my future behavior? Will it be positive or negative?

Isolation, on the other hand, separates us from other people and experiences. Sometimes being isolated isn't something we can control, but more often it is a choice, a negative choice to escape from personal growth in order to live in the past. In a recent report done by the National Academies of Sciences, Engineering and Medicine and sponsored by AARP, the results showed there are higher mortality rates among those who are socially isolated. Even more alarming was the statistic that three in five or 61% of adult U.S. workers, reported being lonely, up five-fold from the previous year. And that was among younger, still employed individuals. Older people and especially those who live alone would show even worse results. These numbers were disturbing because loneliness and social isolation have been estimated to shorten a person's life by fifteen years, which is the equivalent in impact to being obese or smoking fifteen cigarettes per day! Isolation leads to all kinds of health problems like heart disease, high blood pressure and weakened immune system not to mention anxiety and depression. The study added that living alone does not inevitably lead to isolation, but it can be a contributing factor, and the number of people living alone in the United States jumped from thirteen percent in 1950 to twenty-eight percent in 2019. Since older adults are at particular risk of isolation due to retirement and especially widowhood, it is vital to recognize these dangers and do whatever we can to stay mentally healthy and in touch regularly with others. Solitude is a choice we make to think and reflect quietly, but it isn't escapism from the reality of a new station in life. It is not the same as social isolation. After the Corona virus forced us to change the way we lived, I began to realize even more that solitude is always a choice we make. But being forced to stay at home, when there is no one else to share that home, felt more like isolation than solitude. Solitude has, however, provided an opportunity allowing me to have the time to sort it all out and hopefully make healthier decisions about how to proceed from here.

Fifteen

MEMORY VS. NOSTALGIA

As I write this, it is one week until Christmas, my third Christmas without Paul. It is a time for memories to pop up all over the place, and anyone who has lost a partner will agree that the holidays can be difficult. As I think about this new chapter in my life, I have begun to compare two other concepts: memory and nostalgia. Christmas has always been my favorite time of year; I love everything about it, the shopping, the decorating, the lights, the baking, the gift giving and the family time. After my father died in April, my mother was still not dealing well with living alone at Christmas. It took her another year to decide to move in with Paul and me. She wasn't going to put up a Christmas tree for the first time in her life, and I remember I got angry with her for what I perceived as hiding from the holiday. I went over to her townhouse and forced her put up a small tabletop tree and trimmed it with her. She was not happy about doing it, and there were tears, mine angry tears, hers sad tears. She was a prisoner of nostalgia. I regret now that I was so hard on her because after Paul died, the last thing I wanted to do was put up our big family tree, and I finally understood how she had felt.

I did make the decision not to put up our smaller travel tree that held all the ornaments we brought from every city and country we had ever visited. When his memory was starting to fade, I would put all the ornaments on the coffee table and we would take turns trying to remember one fact about that trip. We had lots of good times doing this until the last Christmas of his life when his memory was letting him down, and the effort to remember each trip was too difficult. After he died, I couldn't put up that tree. It was just too painful. But after I bought my new house, I did put it on the screen porch with all the lights and ornaments to stay up all year around because I still enjoyed looking at it, grateful for having seen so much of the world.

My first Christmas as a widow forced me to put up the big family tree because the kids and grandkids would still be coming over, and it had to be done. And I knew since it was probably going to be the last Christmas in that house, they needed it to be like it had always been. My heart wasn't in it, but it got done nonetheless. My sister generously offered to come over and trim the tree with me. "Nobody," she said, "should put up a tree alone." I accepted her offer, but at the last minute she had an emergency and couldn't come. So I turned on the music and decorated the tree by myself. Then I realized something interesting. The thought of doing it alone was worse than the actual doing it. I realized for the last years of Paul's life, I always decorated the tree alone. He sat in the same room supervising, mostly with his eyes closed. So the only thing that was different was that the chair was empty next to the tree. So I invited the dog to take a seat. Perception is a funny thing. By the second Christmas, the first one in the new house, there were new traditions, new decorating and new fun, and I was surprised it went so well. It was in a smaller space, and we were definitely a bit more crowded, but it didn't seem to matter. That last Christmas Paul was alive was a very special one for several reasons. He had had a heart attack the week before, and we weren't sure if he would be alive for Christmas, but he came home from the hospital on the 23rd. As was our custom, we played Joy to the World on the CD player and amped up the volume to kick off the gift exchange time. Paul would always sit in the arm chair, wearing his Santa hat and acting as conductor of the orchestra as the family found their seats on the couch, or the chairs or the floor. I didn't realize that my daughter videotaped him doing that on his last Christmas, and I am so glad she did. I will always watch it every Christmas to hold that memory close to my heart. It's a wonderful memory, no longer quite as painful but more special and precious.

So what is the difference then between memory and nostalgia? They are very much alike but also very different I think. The way I see it is that memory is our way to keep the past as a part of us, to draw on and take pleasure in, or also to bring back bad times and learn from them. I have known people who had a very unhappy childhood, and their memories do not bring back good feelings. They don't want to share them. But memory could also allow them to look back and realize all they survived in spite of it all and hopefully learn how not to repeat the negative in their present life. Having memories is a vital part of being human; it helps us to keep the past alive for the next generation. How many times did my children ask me when they were growing up to tell them a story about when I was a little girl? Too many to count, and I told a lot of stories over the years. Those were my memories of the wonderful childhood I was fortunate to have had. It was important to pass them on. Even my grandchildren asked for those kinds of stories when they were growing up, and I loved sharing them again. I now have fifty years of stories about our marriage and fifty years of fascinating stories about our travels together. But all these memories aren't making me a prisoner of the past. They don't keep me from moving on. Nostalgia, on the other hand, doesn't allow us to do that.

I think we use the word nostalgia too loosely in our society. It isn't just remembering happy times, but rather keeping us stuck in the memory of those happier times, like quicksand, keeping us from being able to step out from the past. It locks us into an unhappy present and keeps us from progressing into a brighter future. It's exactly what my mother was doing. She was stuck in the quicksand of an unhappy present and didn't want or have the energy to pull herself out of it. I do not judge her for this state of mind. I was not ninety when Paul died, and I have no idea what it must have been like for her at that age.

Webster defines nostalgia as a longing for something far away. The key word there, I think, is longing. Are there times when I feel nostalgic about different times? According to his definition, yes sometimes. I get a bit nostalgic during the holidays remembering the fun of buying toys for my little ones, watching them decorate the tree with all the ornaments on the lower branches. I defy any parent to say they don't get nostalgic remembering their children's youth. I defy any widows to say they don't miss the good times with their life partners. When Sesame Street began its fifty year run on TV, my oldest was just a year old. We watched it together twice a day every day. I can still sing all the lyrics to all the songs, and I watched the show with some of my grandchildren as well. Recently, on the fiftieth anniversary of the show, the producers put together a documentary showing many clips from years past. I have to admit I watched it from beginning to end, and yes, there were occasional tears. But I found it interesting, too, that the same year the Kennedy Center Awards also recognized Sesame Street, and I watched it again. When the performers sang those old familiar songs with the Muppets on the stage, the camera panned out to the audience, and there were tears running down many faces. Were we all just longing for our youth, a time of fun and innocence that seemed so far away? Maybe, but that's not the same thing as being mentally stuck in that stage of life. For me and for the members of that audience I suspect, those songs just brought back wonderful, innocent memories to cherish.

The third Christmas without Paul found me decorating my house, baking the dozens of cookies, most to be given away, wrapping all the gifts, playing the holiday music and singing along. I still looked at the lighted travel tree on the porch and remembered all the great trips Paul and I shared. Did I wish he were still here telling stories about each ornament? Of course! Did I wish he were still here to sneak into the kitchen to steal a warm cookie off the cookie sheet? You bet I did. And when we played Joy to the World on Christmas Day, I saw him in my mind's eye conducting the orchestra as the family took their seats. And it was all okay.

But there was one more "first" I did not see coming. My favorite

Mass to attend at this time of year was the Christmas Eve candlelight Mass. It's just a beautiful celebration in a church illuminated only by candles and Christmas tree lights. Every year since Paul died, one or more of my children has gone with me to this Mass. But at this third Christmas without Paul, all three of them had obligations with their in-laws on Christmas Eve. I had never in my life been to a Christmas Mass alone, but there was no way to avoid it. I suppose I could have changed my plans and gone to one of the Masses they attended so as not to be alone, usually on Christmas Eve afternoon with a million screaming children who don't want to be there. I have done that in years past when my own kids were little, and the experience was sorely lacking in that good spiritual feeling! So going alone took me by surprise since I thought I had pretty much experienced all the "firsts" I was going to have. As I took my seat in the pew, I began to look around at all the other people entering the church. So many families all sitting together, parents, and children and grandchildren all filling the pews. So many couples huddled together, some old-old like me but still happily married, some young, obviously still dating, holding hands and snuggling close to each other. But from my vantage point, I didn't see one other person sitting alone, and I admit I had a problem keeping the tears at bay, especially when the beautiful music began. The lyrics stuck in my throat and nothing came out. It was a terrible moment of self-pity until I got myself together. But with some effort it did pass, another "first" conquered. It was a moment of nostalgia that could have swallowed me up and ruined Christmas Eve. I doubt if Paul would have wanted that for me.

So what is the lesson I took away from the third Christmas as a widow? Simply this: my life cannot and will not stop unless I choose to stop it. And even though there will inevitably be tough moments from time to time, I have to acknowledge them and accept them for what they are, but then I must choose to move on, hopefully to create new memories for both my family and me.

-Sixteen-

LEGACY

Life in this twenty-first century seems to be moving so fast with advancing technology. It feels hard to keep pace with it. Sometimes it feels like the present is but a brief minute. I nearly laughed when I heard that the new I-Phone I had just bought was replaced with the latest model...the following day! I was still figuring out all the bells and whistles on my new and now outdated purchase!

I find it quite bizarre that companies like "Ancestry" and "123 and Me" are so incredibly popular right now. As fast as we are moving into the future, what is it about delving into the past years, decades and even centuries that is so inviting? I think there is a real fascination with what came before, what genes were passed down to us, what legacy is in our heritage. Legacy, that's a great word, and since Paul died I began thinking about it.

We learned quite a lot about Paul's ancestry when we took the vacation to Montreal and found the Hurtubise House, a private museum, on the Canadian historic registry. He was descended from two French brothers who left the Loire Valley of France and helped build the old town of Montreal in the 1600's. One was killed in an Indian raid, and the other went on to continue the family name in North America. Someone in Paul's family also researched his roots on his mother's side back to Ireland. It seems they found a rather sketchy man who landed in jail for his rebellious behavior. I firmly believe Paul got a few of those genes! My cousin did quite a bit of research about my roots on my father's side tracing them back to pre-World War II Poland and Germany. And I would love to know anything about my mother's ancestry; unfortunately my sister and I know very little.

I looked up the word "legacy" in the dictionary. Webster gives it two definitions: money or property left to someone in a will and anything handed down as from an ancestor. The former suggests wealth or financial success. The latter is a more open-ended definition. So should we equate legacy with success? Maybe that depends on what you consider success.

Paul's family was never wealthy. When his mother was widowed at a very young age, she had very little to live on since his dad had not bought a life insurance policy. She had not worked outside the home, staying home to bring up five children. She had never learned to drive a car, and she struggled during those early years of widowhood. I'm still not sure how she managed. Paul had to put himself through school and never had much money to spend on dating. I used to kid him that I certainly wasn't marrying him for his money. But when his mother died and he had to give the eulogy, it was filled with stories of her successes as a Christian woman and an encouraging parent. Perhaps tenacity, her values and the will to survive were her legacy to Paul.

My parents were not really wealthy, but we were always comfortable and wanted for nothing. My dad worked hard in a company he began, and my mom was a stay-at-home mom. They had helped my maternal grandmother escape from an abusive marriage by taking her in after a near fatal heart attack. She lived with us until her death at age 80. Because of my parents' gift of longevity, they outlived their investments, and my sister and brother-in-law and Paul and I helped to support them. My father hated taking money from us; he had never allowed himself to be in debt to anyone, but we reminded him that he had helped both of us at different times early in our marriages, and now it was our turn to help them. But it was one of the few times I saw him cry. Later on, they inherited a windfall from one of his sisters, and rather than spend it on themselves, they couldn't wait to give it away to children and grandchildren. I will always remember the night he sat in our kitchen and shared the news of their good fortune. He was nearly giddy with joy. He couldn't wait to pay us back. Their legacy to me was partially financial thanks to his inheritance, but more importantly, I consider their legacy to be an incredible spirit of generosity.

The reason I began thinking about all this after Paul's death was because of all the people who came to his funeral. The visitation was in the church prior to the Mass. It could have gone on much longer than the allotted time because the line was still long when the funeral directors told everyone to find their seats in the pews. Some of that time is a kind of blur now, but I do remember people introducing themselves to me, people who knew Paul years before I did, some sixty years ago and who still wanted to pay their respects after all that time. Some were colleagues he had never mentioned to me but who had a profound respect for him and his work. There were former students who had benefitted from his teaching in the medical school. I heard stories about how he had affected their lives, so many lives from different stages of his life. Later when I read through the guest registry book, I couldn't believe how many people had come. We have a fairly large church, and it was filled to capacity. We never had a lot of money in our fifty years of marriage, but his life was definitely one of success. Even the Hospice nurses talked about how much he had taught them about life during the two years they spent with him. What a legacy!

When I had to clean out his home office in preparation to sell the house after his death, it was necessary to get rid of all his medical tomes; no library wanted old medical books. All his teaching aids went into the garbage can since they were all outdated thanks to advancing technology. It felt like I was throwing out an entire career, and I was so sad and feeling terribly guilty about doing it. But I convinced myself that his legacy wasn't a bunch of old books and notes. It was all the knowledge he had imparted to all those budding scientists who would carry it on for years in their careers.

Our three adult children sometimes mention things about their dad that convince me his legacy is much more than any money they may inherit someday. They talk about his humility, his gentle, soft-spoken nature, his extreme kindness, his generosity to a fault, sometimes to our detriment financially. He had a Ph.D. in a very crucial and relatively new field of medicine, lectured nationally and internationally, but never let anyone less educated than he feel less than he was. He could talk to anybody about anything. I remember after one university cocktail party we attended asking him how he knew so much about something I overheard him discussing with a total stranger. He laughed and said, "I didn't know anything about it, but neither did he!" Our kids may not have realized all those wonderful traits about him when they were growing up, but now as adults, they are well aware of their dad's legacy.

That brings me now to my present state of life. I have to wonder what my legacy will be to my children and my grandchildren. I don't know the answer to that question yet. I know they will have all the songs I have written over the years and recorded on an old audio cassette. All they will have to do is find something to play it on! The grandchildren will have the children's books I have written and shared with them and their classmates. But those are tangibles. I think about my family now and what kind of example I will set for them as I meander through the latter years of my life as a widow. This feels like such a formidable responsibility. I have to get it right. Hopefully, if the family genes pass down, and I make it into the oldest/old category, I'll still have a lot of years left to work on it. I can only hope the legacy I leave will be one they can be proud of. I will try to keep the question of that legacy in the forefront of my mind since it's still a work in progress.

-Seventeen-

FAITH

I f you are a person of faith, then this chapter is for you. I'd like to mull over the part faith and religion play in our lives at various times in our life. Since I have been widowed, it's another issue I have found myself thinking about. And it really doesn't matter what your religion of choice is; if you believe in a Higher Power, regardless of the name you give to Him or Her, you are a person of faith.

I was brought up in the Catholic faith, and the importance of our faith was never in doubt in my family. I have to admit when I look back at my childhood, I was a weird little kid when it came to religion. We went to Catholic schools, taught by nuns; I went to Mass every morning with my elementary school class, learned to sing Gregorian chant and loved every minute of it. I read books given to me by my surrogate grandfather, a Franciscan priest who had officiated at my parents' wedding, about the shrines at Lourdes and Fatima. I wanted terribly to have my own miraculous vision by Mary, but much to my dismay, that never happened. I had an aunt who was a Franciscan nun, whom we visited at her convent house occasionally. When other kids had stamp collections, I had a collection of Holy Cards. I was given statues of Christ or of St. Anne, my Patron Saint, for gifts at birthdays. I even created an altar in my bedroom with these statues, my rosary, and prayer book. At the time, none of this seemed out of the ordinary to me, but in retrospect, I'm sure none of my friends had this same kind of preoccupation with religion.

When I graduated from an all-girls Catholic high school in 1962, there were fifteen in my class who entered the convent. I found out later that there were many girls who were surprised when I didn't join them. The fact is I did think about it for a while; I even put my half-slip on my head to see what I'd look like in a veil! I thought at one time I wanted to be a missionary and work with the Franciscans in New Mexico teaching the Indians, but gave up on that idea eventually.

I was in high school and college in the 1960's when Vatican II was creating all kinds of upheaval in the Catholic Church. Mass began to be said in English instead of Latin, and when Paul and I got married in 1967, we had one of the first English wedding Masses in our parish. Paul had spent a few years in the seminary at Notre Dame University in South Bend, Indiana but didn't stay long enough to be ordained. Their loss was my gain! He was a deeply spiritual man, and our views on most things were the same, except on one very troubling issue…birth control. Of course the Catholic faith banned all kinds of birth control, and I had never bucked the system in my life, but this was a real challenge for me since Paul didn't buy into the Church's thinking on this issue. After having three babies in five years, I had a talk with my confessor (re-read the chapter on guilt) who shocked me when he said he was quite sure I wouldn't burn in hell if I went to the pharmacy when I left the confessional!

When you're working full time and have a house, husband and three kids, religion can end up being put on the back burner except for going to Mass on Sunday. But I tried to get the family involved in our weekend Mass by starting a guitar group which provided the music for the liturgy on Saturday, Paul was a Lector and Distributer of the Eucharist, our son was a server and occasionally our daughters sang with me. I wanted the children to eventually realize that you get out of the Mass what you put into it. It's not meant to be an hour to be entertained. At that time in my life, singing was how I prayed best. Music has always moved me and still does. We did this weekly ritual for ten years until we moved out of that parish. By then I welcomed the anonymity.

I also taught French in a public high school where church and state had to remain far apart. I made no secret of the fact that I was Catholic, my students knew where I stood on most things, and occasionally this became an issue. French class gave me an outlet since you can't teach French history without teaching church history. They are completely entwined. I had to be very careful in class not to cross any lines. But Paul and I took seven trips to France with my students over the course of my career and visited many cathedrals along the way including the Papal Palace in Avignon. All these trips opened the door for lots of conversations about religion, and since the school didn't sponsor these trips, Paul and I could say anything we wanted about our faith. As a former seminarian, he could present a view of Catholicism unique from mine. One of the students actually asked him about what life in the seminary was like. I learned years later that this student, who had not grown up with any religion at all, had converted to Catholicism.

When my mother became a widow in 2001, her faith remained very strong, but as I wrote in an earlier chapter, she could no longer find solace in her parish church. My parents had even donated money to pay for a pew that still has their names on it. But she could no longer go there without him; it was just too painful. Her faith never wavered, but she wasn't ever completely comfortable in my parish either. I used to take her every Sunday, and especially during Lent we went to one additional Mass each week. Of course she never missed Good Friday services. After her death in 2006, I was having my own crisis of faith.

She had died in September, 2006, and the following Lent, I was missing her terribly. At the Good Friday service, I was sitting alone in the pew, wallowing in my own stew of grief, and had a moment of very negative questioning. I remember thinking, *what if all this religion stuff is nothing but a load of garbage? What if there is no Heaven? What if I'll really never see her again in the next life, if there even is a next life?* It was such a moment of depression I couldn't finish the service, got up and drove home in tears. I ran into the house and was up just about two steps when the overpowering aroma of her perfume filled the air. It literally dropped me to my knees. I sat on the steps, taking in the familiar memory of her wonderful fragrance and had to laugh. I remember saying out loud, "Okay, I hear you. I'm sorry. Shame on me; I won't think those kinds of thoughts anymore."

During Paul's long illness, especially during those last four difficult years of caregiving, I was on my knees more times than I can count. Sometimes it felt like my faith was all I had to grab onto. I have a strong faith in St. Anne, my Patron Saint, and I was making a novena to her for nine days before her feast day, July 26th. Paul had told his Hospice nurse that he knew he was dying but asked her not to tell me. She honored that request even though in my heart I knew it, too. I had been praying for strength to know how to care for him, or to take him if it was his time to go. On her feast day, July 26th, he told me he was "checking out". He knew it was time to tell me the end was near. He died two days later. I may not have had a Heavenly apparition of Mary, but I believe I had a Heavenly intercession. And when he died in 2017, I had requested certain music for his funeral service. One song in particular helped me through that day; the song was *In This Very Place, Jesus is in this very place*. It was terribly emotional to hear and even though I couldn't get my voice to sing the words, those lyrics comforted me.

I had to think of my mother when I went to church without him for the first time after he died. As I wrote in the epilogue of my first memoir, *In Sickness and in Health*, "We had gone to the same Mass every Sunday, saw the same friendly, welcoming people, thanked the same man who opened the door for me as I pushed the wheelchair through, and sat in the same pew reserved for the handicapped. That first Sunday without Paul, I felt like I had a bull's eye on my back with the word WIDOW in the center. I felt like I was missing a limb; I couldn't decide where to sit; I got terribly choked trying to sing. All I could think about was how I used to cherish the infrequent times when Paul would try to sing. That was an awful morning and not a very good spiritual experience. I couldn't wait to leave church, and I cried all the way home.

The following week, I decided to get smart and go to the Saturday evening Mass where no one would even recognize me. It is commonplace in our parish to have a baby baptized right after the homily, and the entire congregation then welcomes this new little Christian into the fold. But never have I witnessed a marriage in the middle of a weekend Mass. Unfortunately, for me, there was going to be a wedding ceremony taking place after the homily. At the entrance hymn, the priest, servers and lectors processed in as always, but they were followed by the wedding attendants and the beautiful bride in her long white dress and flowing veil and looking as radiant as only a bride can look. My immediate reaction was to think, *I remember how I felt walking down the aisle fifty years ago. You're just beginning your marriage, and I just ended mine.* I got up and practically ran out of the church and barely made it to the door before the tears came in torrents. I couldn't get to my car fast enough, and then came the ugly cry, the moments of feeding the bad wolf until there were no more tears to give him. My daughters invited me to go to Mass with them the following week, and for a brief moment I considered it. But then I thought I would be relying on them to keep me together. This was something I had to do alone."

This must have been how my mother had felt as a new widow going back to her church without her husband. Once again, just like when she didn't want to put up a Christmas tree, I began to understand. Of course, I did manage to get through this tough time of going to church without Paul, but it took some time.

Paul and I had always enjoyed going to a service called Taize, a kind of repetitive chanting prayer that originated in Taize, France. Our parish held this service only twice a year, in Advent and in Lent. The church is lighted with candles only, providing a calm atmosphere conducive to meditation and quiet reflection. I went to the service the first Advent after Paul died, and couldn't find the calm, couldn't get into the meditative chant and left feeling absolutely nothing. I hated it, and that bothered me. I was afraid I was losing my ability to relate to my faith in the same way as before. After another year, I tried it again and found it easier, not great but easier. I could only hope that this decrease in Taize inspiration would eventually go away.

My faith continues to give me comfort when I need it, and I honestly don't know how people get through the many crises of life without some kind of spiritual life on which to fall back. But I also have come to realize that the state of our lives at any given time is a contributing factor to how our faith plays out or doesn't play out in our day to day activities; it ebbs and flows with the tough times and the good times. I feel certain that God is well aware of all of this. It's okay. I know my faith has continued to evolve since I began this new phase of life as a widow. I no longer have an altar in my bedroom, but I will continue to see my faith as my lifeline and my anchor to get through whatever comes next. I may have begun widowhood singing *The Lord Hears the Cry of the Poor,* but if I must choose a song to motivate me now, music to lift me up when I need it, to define this next chapter, it will most certainly be *Sing a New Song Unto the Lord.*

EPILOGUE

So what are the lyrics, and what is the theme of my new song? What I have discovered is that my way to plow through this difficult time, especially the year of emotional firsts, was to attack it head on, make my lists and get it done! That may not be right for anyone else, and that's okay. That's how I started my new song. I discovered that even though change is hard, it can bring about a profound sense of peace once it is accomplished, when the heart is open to it. The first time I had to publicly acknowledge the fact that I was a widow and that my situation was not going to change nearly brought me to my knees. I had to make the decision that widowhood may have been the last word on the line of the medical form, but it was not the end of the line for me. I came to realize that just because the first year was finished, there would still occasionally be "firsts" I didn't see coming, like the first social gathering as "just me" instead of Paul and me or the first Christmas Mass alone. They were difficult moments but also moments I survived.

I found myself contemplating the difference between the words "lonely" and "alone" understanding they are not synonymous, and it was an enormous relief to acknowledge that I was at peace with being alone. Examining the difference between the words "isolation" and "solitude" forced me to dig deep into my heart and choose to accept the benefits of solitude even though there were times when isolation felt easier. Comments about getting involved romantically again forced me to examine why those comments upset me so much and convinced me I was content being unattached.

I remembered all the guilt I felt after Paul died, guilt for not always being as kind and compassionate as I should have been in his last years, but finally recognizing it is vitally important to forgive ourselves, too. I was also able to put to rest the guilt I felt for deciding not to return to the cemetery after those difficult moments of self-analysis.

Physical discomforts from falling, getting stomach ulcers, breaking ribs and struggling through physical therapy have taught me to take better care of myself, especially now that I am alone, to do the work necessary to improve and accept the inevitable personal physical limitations of age and, more importantly, the humility that has accompanied them.

Finding the right words to help friends who have lost their other halves has been one of the most gratifying results of having gone before them in widowhood. When my good friend and Paul's Hospice nurse lost her husband unexpectedly just a month ago, she called me at 10:30 P.M. to talk. I sensed after that conversation that she needed me to be with her at his funeral. It was going to be at a church an hour away from my home. This woman who had gotten me through so many tough times now seemed to need me to help her through her first days of anguish. The relief on her face when she saw me enter the church humbled me. I felt blessed as our relationship had come full circle.

I have spent time reflecting on the difference between the words "memory" and "nostalgia", becoming grateful for the lessons my mother taught me on how not to grieve, but also to recognize how she felt with more compassion. Some of the best advice my mother ever gave me was to "not grow old regretting the things you didn't try out of fear". Those words came back to me as I struggled with my fear of traveling alone, and they nudged me forward. Memories of fifty years with Paul are certainly a mixed bag of emotions. As I wrote earlier, so many of the dreams I had about him in the beginning were unhappy, stressful, reliving difficult moments. Very few were good dreams. But as time went on more dreams of him were happy, when he was very young, some even before we were married. I wake up grateful for the experience. While talking to my daughter recently, she shared that she had been having many dreams about her dad, dreams of him as a younger man, not yet sick when he still had the twinkle in his eyes. But then she would wake up and remember how he was at the end, and it made her sad. It had been such a long time since she had seen that healthy dad, and it made her miss him even more. I told her about my recent dreams, and I chose to see it as a message from him. Maybe since we were both having these "young Paul" dreams, he was trying to tell us both to remember him like that and to forget how he deteriorated at the end. She was getting stuck in nostalgia, and I wanted both of us to embrace the good memories.

Lastly, widowhood has forced me to rediscover my purpose, to remember the new philosophy of life I adopted after retirement, that is, to do something good for someone else, something good for my body, my mind, and my soul each day. It has forced me to take a good look at my relationship with God and the role my faith continues to play in my life. It has forced me to think about the meaning of "legacy" and accept the powerful responsibility it brings with it. I hope my legacy to my children and grandchildren will be, in part, these thoughts and conclusions I have reached as I meander through the mountains and valleys of my widowhood. This legacy, this work in progress, will be my new song.

READER'S GUIDE

Do you think faith plays a role in the grief process and if so, how?

Do you have a support system as you face this time of life?

What role does your support system play in helping you adjust?

Were there any "unanticipated firsts" you experienced after being widowed?

Do you consider yourself an introvert or an extrovert?

What role do these self-descriptive terms play in your adjustment to being widowed?

How are you approaching the first tasks facing you regarding widowhood?

Have dreams of your spouse affected your waking hours? If so, how do you deal with that?

What lessons have you learned about yourself since becoming widowed?

What advice would you give to someone else facing this new role based on your experience?

Printed in the United States
By Bookmasters